SULLY

THE EPIC LIFE & FOOTBALL LEGEND OF COACH BOB SULLIVAN

ALSO BY JEFF APPELQUIST

NONFICTION

Earthrise: Leadership Lessons From the Apollo Space Missions

Changing Places: Travels in a Vanishing World

Legacy of Excellence: A Centennial History of the Toro Company

Wisdom Is Not Enough: Reflections on Leadership & Teams

*Sacred Ground: Leadership Lessons from
Gettysburg & the Little Bighorn*

FICTION

The Great Wild West: An American Journey

SULLY

THE EPIC LIFE & FOOTBALL LEGEND OF COACH BOB SULLIVAN

JEFF APPELQUIST

ISBN-13: 978-1-63489-799-0

Cover and interior design by Emily Rodvold.

Printed in the United States of America
First Printing: 2025

29 28 27 2625   5 4 3 2 1

WISE INK

Wise Ink Creative Publishing
807 Broadway St. NE, Suite 46
Minneapolis, MN 55413
www.wiseink.com

To all Carleton Knight football players
Past, present & future
Whose warrior spirit & fraternal bonds are forever
As the great King Henry V proclaimed (according to the Bard) to steel his soldiers' hearts
on the eve of the Battle of Agincourt in 1415,
"We shall be remembered, we few, we happy few, we band of brothers
For he today that sheds his blood with me shall be my brother…"
The British archers, vastly outnumbered but profoundly inspired by their heroic leader,
went bravely forth, filled the sky with their arrows,
and cut down the flower of French chivalry and young manhood
to win a great victory
GO KNIGHTS!

THIS IS THE BEGINNING OF A NEW DAY

By Heartsill Wilson

"This is the beginning of a new day.
God has given me this day to use as I will.
I can waste it or use it for good.
What I do today is very important because I am exchanging a day of my life for it.
When tomorrow comes, this day will be gone forever,
leaving something in its place I have traded for it.
I want it to be a gain, not a loss – good not evil.
Success, not failure,
in order that I shall not regret the price I paid for it.
Because the future is just
a whole string of nows."

Team Prayer that Coach Sullivan required his players to memorize
They recited it together every game day Saturday in the fall

Table of Contents

Prologue: Origins   *1*

1. The Sullivans   5
2. The Central Catholic High Queensmen   11
3. Gags & the St. John's University Johnnies   18
4. The Hill Pioneers & Cooper Hawks   28
5. Renaissance Man: Poetry & Music   38
6. Football Teaches Life: The Psychology of Winning   46
7. The Creation of a Game & the Carleton College Knights   52
8. Football Gods: Holtz & Walsh   61
9. The Ultimate Chess Match: Philosophy & Schemes   71
10. 1979: Beginnings   83
11. Opening Moves to Middle Game   92
12. Our World Has Stopped   104
13. 1992: Champions   112
14. And Baseball Too   120
15. Endgame to Checkmate   128
16. Bubba & the Northfield Raiders   139
17. Man of Letters: Knights of the Gridiron   147
18. Love & Loss   154
19. Sully & Me   161
20. The Pantheon: Sully's All-Time Knights Team, 1979-2000   172

Epilogue: Legacy   *197*
Acknowledgements & Photos   *206*
Bibliography   *208*
Name Index   *210*

Origins

"I'm all about a small town.
I think it's a great place to grow up."

KACEY MUSGRAVES - COUNTRY WESTERN SINGER

Marshall, Minnesota is a lovely small town. It is, technically, a city but still exudes the look, feel, warmth, and charm of a small town. Marshall sits just over 150 miles southwest of the Twin Cities of Minneapolis and St. Paul. It is a mere hour-long drive directly west to Brookings, just across the South Dakota border. A traveler can get on Highway 19 in Marshall, head east and, eventually, after a scenic journey featuring endless farmland and one sleepy, idyllic little community after another, drive straight into the heart of Northfield, Minnesota, another small town, whose motto is "Cows, Colleges & Contentment." Northfield is famous for the day in September 1876 when local townsfolk, many of them Civil War veterans, sniffed some suspicious activity, got all riled up, then proceeded to shoot Jesse James and his notorious band of outlaws to bloody pieces, thwarting their brazen attempt to rob the First National Bank. Northfield is also home to two esteemed liberal arts colleges: St. Olaf and Carleton.

Marshall is busy and prosperous, with a population of around 14,000. It is the county seat of Lyon County, a railroad center, and a hub for commercial activity. One can pick up a colorful and slickly produced brochure entitled,

"Visit Marshall: Cultivate the Best Experiences" at the Lyon County Historical Museum. The town's motto is "Only in Marshall," and the brochure describes everything a visitor needs to know about what to see and do. There is an abundance of restaurants, hotels and shopping venues. More than a dozen parks and athletic complexes, on 150 total acres, dot the landscape. Memorial Park downtown, which honors the nation's veterans, also displays a beam from the rubble of the 9/11 attack on the World Trade Center. There are numerous hiking and biking trails. The Redwood River, which is a tributary of the mighty Minnesota River and has been known to cause periodic flooding over the years, winds its way through town. Each May Marshall hosts the "Made in Minnesota" beer and wine festival. An excellent farmers market, with locally grown produce from surrounding farms, runs from July to October. In August, the Lyon County Fair features a professional rodeo, a demolition derby and live bands. The citizens of Marshall are proud of their own institution of higher learning, Southwest Minnesota State University, almost 9,000 students strong, whose campus occupies more than 200 acres in the northeast corner of town.

The good people of Marshall are also deeply conscious of their history, not all of it bright. The first settlers established their new community in 1872, naming it after William Rainey Marshall, who served as the fifth governor of Minnesota from 1866 to 1870. Among many other experiences in a supremely eventful life, Marshall saw serious combat duty in the Civil War and as a lieutenant colonel of the Seventh Minnesota Volunteer Regiment in the Dakota War of 1862. This horrific event still haunts the distant collective memory of many Minnesotans, especially those who reside in the western part of the state.

Out of grievances aplenty, Dakota Indian frustration and anger culminated in a violent uprising in August 1862. As many as 700 innocent white settlers were massacred, with tens of thousands more terrified people displaced from their homes. The U.S. Army intervened to quell the violence. More than 500 Indians, many of them also innocent women and children, died during the conflict and in the aftermath. Thirty-eight Dakota men, convicted as the primary perpetrators, were hung all at once, in Mankato, Minnesota, on the day after Christmas, 1862, in the largest mass execution in U.S. history. For the intrepid founders of Marshall, this dark and anguishing tragedy happened right in their own backyard and only one decade earlier.

Marshall continued to expand as the years went by, serving as a regional nexus for the agricultural and railroad industries. Construction of new rail lines connected Marshall to larger markets. By the late 1930s the population sat at around 4,500. By 1950, it had expanded to almost 6,000. Because it was the county seat and clearly the most populated place for miles around, kids growing up during that era did not necessarily think of it as a small town. There was plenty to do, friends were abundant, and you could safely walk or ride a bike anywhere, anytime. Sure, everybody knew everybody; Emmanuel Kant is supposed to have said," The nice thing about living in a small town is that when you don't know what you're doing, someone else does," which was as true in Marshall as anywhere. But young people in the '40s and '50s still thought Marshall, Minnesota was a pretty damn fine place to grow up.

For sports-loving boys in Marshall there were opportunities in both school and city leagues to play football as the leaves turned gorgeous shades and temperatures cooled in the fall; to go inside the local gym to play basketball when the weather turned nasty and snowy and cold in winter; and to play baseball in the warm, bright sunshine of summer. When they weren't involved in organized athletics, groups of friends picked teams and played sandlot or pickup ball, sometimes challenging the guys in the next neighborhood over for bragging rights.

For one group of boys, close pals all, when they were not involved in some kind of athletic contest, a favorite activity was to head over to the Roxie Theater on Main Street and take in a Saturday matinee. A ticket cost a dime - big money back then - and the boys loved comedies starring characters such as Bob Hope, or the Marx Brothers, or Bud Abbott and Lou Costello. They would enjoy a shoot-'em-up John Wayne western, like *Red River*, *Fort Apache*, or *She Wore a Yellow Ribbon*. Or maybe they would watch Jimmy Cagney or Humphrey Bogart in a crime thriller.

For one boy, however, who was born in Marshall in 1937, the movie itself was not the most interesting part of the show. Instead, he sat riveted by the newsreels that always preceded the main attraction. The newsreels were short films that combined journalism and entertainment and were primarily about current events of the day. Many of them featured sports updates. The newsreels that showed football clips, and especially footage of the mighty Notre Dame Fighting Irish, fascinated this boy to no end.

From 1940 to 1949, the Irish compiled a record of 82-9-6. Frank Leahy was their famous coach, and they were nearly unbeatable. The boy knew the names of all the Notre Dame stars of that era: Angelo Bertelli, a tailback and quarterback, won the first of Notre Dame's many Heisman Trophies in 1943; Johnny Lujack won the Heisman in 1947 while quarterbacking the Irish to an undefeated 9-0 season and the national title; Leon Hart, who was a massive 6 foot 5 inch, nearly 260-pound end and fullback, took home the Heisman in 1949.

There was something in the newsreels about the glamor of these legendary names, the design and intricacies of their myriad battle formations, the speed and deftness of the plays they ran, the contest of wills and intense chess match between opposing coaches, the sound and fury and excitement and violence of the action, that simply mesmerized the boy. He determined, as a pre-adolescent, before he ever shaved, that he would someday be the head football coach at Notre Dame. He did not achieve that goal, but football coaching was the profession he would pursue, and he never deviated from his chosen career path.

He was a slight boy with a soft voice, but mighty in energy and spirit, in the beginnings of a passionate lifelong love affair with sports, most especially football.

His name was Bob Sullivan.

CHAPTER 1

The Sullivans

"Love is never defeated, and I could add, the history of Ireland proves it."

POPE JOHN PAUL II

The Sullivan family odyssey begins like so many others, as a story about immigrants, and dreams of a better life in the land of opportunity. They came to America, via England, from Ireland. In 2009, Bob Sullivan wrote a concise, 80-page history of his family, focusing on the paternal side. He called his little treatise, *The Sullivans' Journey: Ireland to America*. In his forward he explained, "This work is based on the theory that you have to know where you've been before you can know where you're going."

The origins of the project began in 2007 when Sully accompanied his daughter Molly and her husband on a trip to Ireland. Sully recalled, "I had intended to go to Ireland soon after I retired at the end of 2000, but something always prevented my going. We went in May and of course, I loved it." They succeeded in locating the county, towns, church and burial plots of several Hanlons, who were kinfolk to Bob's paternal grandmother Elizabeth. But otherwise, efforts to dig further into family history, including visits to genealogy offices in Dublin and elsewhere, ended in frustration.

When he got back home, Bob vowed to continue his research. He wrote, "With the help of a friend who was in fact a genealogist, I was able to uncover a great deal more information over the summer. My aversion to the computer made this task unwieldy, to say the least, but eventually through typical Irish perseverance, stubbornness, and some Irish luck, my passion for pursuit of the Sullivan genealogy project took flight and it has possessed me ever since… The emigration from Ireland, the tragic history of the Irish, particularly the Irish Catholics, really caught my interest. In many respects we are lucky to be here at all. It is only through the faith, vision and fortitude of Peter and Anna [Bob's great grandparents] that we have come to be."

Sully explored in detail some of the many reasons people like his great grandparents chose to leave Ireland: "Overpopulation, grinding poverty, high rents, excessive land subdivision, unemployment, agrarian violence, periodic crop failures, typhus epidemics, and religious and political disputes made Ireland a country of little opportunity and great despair. The failure of the potato crops between 1845-1852 added famine to the list and precipitated heavy emigration… The spirit of adventure or the simple wish to escape the stifling effect of the religious and moral regime in Ireland in the aftermath of the great famine were also incentives to go abroad."

Bob also identified what he thought were the best attributes that the Irish who came to America brought with them: "The Irish were superb wordsmiths, poets, writers, musicians, jovial, possessed of a real love of religion, family, music and of course 'the drink.'"

Bob's great grandparents, Peter and Anna Sullivan, did not join the epic potato famine migration to America, but instead took a different path. Peter, who was probably born in 1837, was from County Cavan in the province of Ulster and, specifically, from Knockbride parish, located between the townlands of Tuliwatry and Ballieborough. Bob informed us that, "The Irish, the Sullivans included, did not pay homage to accurate dates (PARTICULARLY IF IT RELATED TO GOVERNMENT) [his emphasis]. Whether from the aforementioned mistrust of any government or downright stubbornness – take your pick – Peter Sullivan's birth date is in question."

Anna Loftus was born in 1845, at the very outset of the Great Famine.

She hailed from the province of Connaught and County Galway, near the town of Galway in the West. Her birth name was Honor, but in future censuses and legal documents, she was alternately listed as Anna, Anne, Annie, Ann, and Anora. It appears that Anna was her preferred name. There is some evidence that she remained illiterate throughout her life.

At some point Peter and Anna crossed the Irish Sea to Liverpool, England, where they both appear in the 1861 census. Anna was 16 years old and lived with her mother and an older brother. Peter also lived in Lancashire County, Liverpool, in St. Mathews Parish, as a border with a local family. The census lists him as 23 years old (give or take a year or two). Sully explained, "This tight Irish Catholic enclave in Liverpool made it easy for the Irish to socialize, fall in love and ultimately marry, which is exactly what Peter and Anna did in 1861, sometime between April and June. What Peter and Anna did for a living is anybody's guess. While farming was what Peter knew, chances are he hired out on local farms or farms owned by immigrant Irish."

Eleven children were born to Peter and Anna and nine survived. The two that they lost probably died in England, either at birth or shortly thereafter. Two boys, one born in 1866, the other in 1868, survived. The Sullivans spent at least 11 years in England, at which time they had saved sufficient money for Peter to make the long journey to the United States. Anna and the children would join him as soon as possible.

Peter boarded the *U.S.M. Baltic* in Liverpool, took to his berth in the steerage section, and endured the difficult ocean crossing, arriving ashore in New York City on May 6, 1872. The *Baltic* was typical of the many vessels that transported countless numbers of immigrants, especially during this period in American history, from the old country to the promised land (the author's own two grandfathers made just such a trip, from Sweden, in the early 1900s.) The *Baltic* was a formidable, if not beautiful, ship. She was of iron construction with a giant funnel amidship, and three masts rigged for sail. She had capacity for 100 undoubtedly quite comfortable first-class passengers and 750 undoubtedly packed-like-sardines steerage passengers. When not under sail she was steam powered by a screw propeller and could achieve the not terribly impressive speed of ten knots, making for a long and tedious voyage.

Anna had a third son soon after Peter's departure. She traveled aboard the *S. S. Canada* to America with the boys, and one can only imagine the incredible discomfort they endured in the steerage compartment. They arrived in New York on August 26, 1873. Peter was no doubt happy to see his new son for the first time, and the rest of his loved ones as well. They spent a relatively brief period in New York City, probably in the immigrant Irish enclave of Brooklyn. Then, like so many myriad others looking to improve their fortunes, they took a train and traveled west.

The next official mention of the Sullivans is when a fourth son was born, in November of 1874 in Clinton, Iowa. For approximately five years, the family lived in Benton County, near the town of Vinton in eastern Iowa. A fifth child, and the first female, came along in March 1876. Bob Sullivan's grandfather, Martin John, was born on November 1, 1879, also in Benton County. After Martin's birth the family moved further west to Rock Valley, Iowa. Three more children were born between 1882 and 1889. Anna gave birth to her last child when Peter was 52 (or thereabouts) and she was 45. One can imagine, at that point, Anna had about had it. There is a surviving photograph of her, circa 1905 when she was around 60. She is plain and unsmiling, yet she does not have the look of an old woman. She projects sturdy pioneer vigor. Her eyes are intense as she stares at the camera but nevertheless appear as if they may once have been lovely and fetching. But now, in this photo, the eyes are tinged with world-weariness and even a hint of sadness.

In the 1880 census Peter listed his occupation as "Farmer." Apparently, he had an entrepreneurial bent and some success at buying and then reselling farmland for a profit. Bob wrote, "A deed record uncovered showed that Peter had purchased 160 acres in Sioux County for $1,760.00 in 1891. Chances are that he had farmed and sold at least two other farms as he moved westward through Iowa. Also, in October of 1891 in the District Court of Lyon County, Iowa, Peter became a naturalized citizen of the United States. From 1790 until 1922, a wife automatically became naturalized when her husband obtained citizenship. So, Anna was also in the fold as were all the children." The dream of every immigrant family became official: the Sullivans were American citizens.

Bob continued his research and discovered exactly how the Sullivans ended up in Marshall, Minnesota: "In July of 1901, Peter filed a Quit Claim deed and sold the farm... for the sum of $15,000. This figure netted a $13,240 profit for Peter and Anna over the 10 years that they owned and farmed the property. In 1901-02 that was a tidy sum. Peter was 64 and Anna was 56. They were through farming. They purchased a home at 205 East Main Street (still standing) for $1,800 – a good deal – right? He also purchased a farm in Stanley Township between Marshall and Cottonwood for $9,600." The Sullivans lived peacefully in Marshall for the remainder of their days.

Anna died at the age of 68 on November 11, 1913, of what the doctors called "cancer of the bowels." She was buried in the Calvary Cemetery in Marshall. Peter lived on. A photograph from around 1915 shows him seated in an ornately carved wooden chair, outside on a sunny day, probably on his Stanley Township farm property, as he sits in a field of grass with a small outbuilding in the background. He is stout, with massive thighs, not overweight but not underfed either. He looks formidable and not to be trifled with, as if in a later era he may have made a very mean-spirited and disruptive noseguard on one of his great grandson's football teams. His gray-bearded face projects a serene strength.

Peter died suddenly of a heart attack on February 1, 1919. He is also buried in the Calvary Cemetery, next to his Anna. His obituary in the local paper said of him, "Mr. Sullivan was of quiet, cheerful disposition, and was held in high esteem by all who knew him. He was a devoted husband and father and his kindly manner won for him a large circle of friends. In spite of his advanced age Mr. Sullivan had always enjoyed good health and carried his years well." Family lore has it that Peter did indeed have a substantial contingent of pals, and that in his retirement he liked nothing more than to spend time hoisting a pint or two and playing pool with the boys at the local watering hole. He was a backslapping, storytelling, hale-fellow-well-met kind of guy who was a beloved friend to a lot of people. They missed him when he was gone.

Bob Sullivan's grandfather, Martin John, known as M.J., married Elizabeth, known as Lizzie Hanlon, who was from Inwood, Iowa, on September 11, 1901. Bob related that at the time of their marriage, "M.J. was 22 years old and Lizzie was 17 though she wrote down 19 on the marriage certificate. (Was M.J. 'robbing the cradle?')" Bob also speculated that the wedding celebration unfolded in the grand Irish tradition: "I am certain that plenty of money was spent and lots of food was consumed and who knows about 'the drink?'" Fortunately for M.J. and Lizzie, Peter had generously allowed them to rent and farm the property he purchased in Stanley Township. They were together, they had a livelihood, and the next generation of the Sullivan family was in Marshall to stay.

CHAPTER 2

The Central Catholic High Queensmen

*"It's not how big you are
but how big you play."*

JOHN WOODEN

Robert Arthur Sullivan was born on March 20, 1937, in Marshall, "in an apartment above a bar," he is proud to say with a smile. He is Irish after all.

"When I was born, I developed something called pyloric stenosis, they tell me." Pyloric stenosis is a condition where the opening between the stomach and small intestine thickens, blocking food from entering the intestine. It occurs most often in babies, especially males, who are less than six months old. It can cause vomiting, dehydration and weight loss. And the poor little fella can't tell anyone what's wrong. Left untreated it can be fatal. Fortunately, even in the late 1930s, the condition could be cured with a surgical procedure that corrects the obstruction. "I was not doing well at all, and I was rushed to the Mayo Clinic. They opened up my stomach to save my life, so to speak. My mom and dad jokingly said, 'You were dead on arrival.'"

Bob's parents were Emmet and Lorraine Sullivan. Emmet Eugene Sullivan was born in Marshall on July 10, 1906. He was the third of 13 children of M.J. and Lizzie Sullivan. Big families are a Sullivan tradition: among the 11 of M.J. and Lizzie's children who married, 61 offspring were born. Emmet finished eighth grade but work and earning a living were paramount. He spent a brief period employed in a bakery before becoming a truck driver for the bulk of his career, hauling cargo for various firms. During World War II, he spent two years working as a civilian on the Alaskan pipeline. Later in his professional life he sold cars.

Lorraine Lambert was born on July 21, 1912, also in Marshall. Her family originally came from Quebec, Canada. In the late 1800s they migrated to the United States and began to farm, first in Illinois and then South Dakota, eventually ending up in Marshall. Lorraine's father, Arthur Lambert, died young, at age 41, of a heart attack. Her mother, Eva Suprenant Lambert, now a widow, worked various jobs to support Lorraine and her two younger siblings. Somewhere along the way, probably when they were just kids, Lorraine met Emmet, and they married (guess where) in Marshall, on August 8, 1932. Lorraine also had only an eighth-grade education and spent many years after her marriage working as a photographer's assistant. She also worked for a brief time in the same bakery as Emmet, and as a waitress at the Minnesota Café. Between the two of them, while their income was modest, and they never actually owned their own home until Bob was away at college, Emmet and Lorraine did a fine job over the years of supporting their growing brood.

"My parents were great, as far as I was concerned," reflected Bob. "They were not overly affectionate, which maybe was more the custom in those days. They never went around saying 'I love you' like we do nowadays. They worked. Mom took time off when she was pregnant, but otherwise they just worked hard. But they knew how to have fun too. They liked to go out dancing together."

Four more children, all girls, eventually came along. Sharon Ann was born a year behind Bob in 1938; Nancy Ellen was born in 1943; Rosemary

Lee in 1946; and the family baby, Linda Marie, in 1953. Sully has always very much liked women, and he loves his sisters, all of whom are alive and well as of this writing. But at a point in time, the all-girl thing became simply intolerable for a big brother. He recalled that as a teenager, when his last sister was born, "We were playing basketball in Adrian. It was probably halftime or something and they called me over. 'Your mom just had a baby. I said, 'Well, what?' They said it was another girl. And I said, 'Another girl?! What good is that?'" (Sully's son, Bubba, said that whenever the five siblings would get together at family events over the years, "The four sisters sit there and talk, talk, talk. He doesn't say a word. And then, suddenly, they all turn and gang up on him. It's just hilarious.")

Bob attended the Holy Redeemer Elementary School on Main Street from first through eighth grade. During that time, he became completely enamored with the human drama of athletic competition. His parents did not follow sports; neither of them was athletic (except maybe on the dance floor) so that's not where the fascination began. Bob said, "They never attended a game of any kind until they came to see me play." But when he saw the Notre Dame newsreels at the Roxie, he was hooked, and football became his first love. "The newsreels just made it exciting. I was captivated from the get-go by football. I just romantically fell in love with the game."

He was never a big kid physically, but he was confident in his abilities. His athletic career began when he started playing baseball, as a catcher, in a city summer league at around age 10. Baseball was a big deal in Marshall, the games were played at Legion Field, and the various programs were extremely well organized and popular. Then it was football for Holy Redeemer in the fall, where Bob played quarterback; next was basketball in the winter where he immediately starred as a guard. He developed into an early version of today's point guard: he could pass – and enjoyed directing the action - as well as shoot the ball. He remembered a pivotal event: "Marshall High School had a really good basketball team, and people would flock there on Friday nights to watch them play. At halftime, little kids would go out and play in front of the crowd. Well, I was one of them. And I remember I made a couple of baskets, and the crowd roared." Basketball was clearly his best sport.

It is interesting to note that all three of the positions Bob played - baseball catcher, football quarterback, and basketball guard - involved handling the ball on virtually every play, controlling the game, commanding his teammates, and being at the center of the competition. Sports fans know that the players who are the best at those respective positions are like coaches on the field.

In addition to sports, Sully had work obligations as well, but there was a problem with that: "Okay, I got fired from a lot of jobs back then. I was never interested in working. I was more interested in playing. I overheard my parents talking one time. They said, 'What are we going to do with this kid? We put him in a job as a grocery boy. He got fired there. And he talks to people all the time. He talks too much. What the heck?' I remember one time they got me a job with a produce company. You had to lift bananas and potatoes off box cars and stuff. I was 130 pounds. I could not lift those. The bananas came in a stack like six-feet high. I could not lift that thing. I lasted two days. That was the end of that... So yeah, I was a different breed, apparently, from what most employers were used to dealing with."

The challenge was not necessarily poor performance of job duties or tardiness. "No, the issue was I was too inquisitive. I would talk to people all the time. 'Who are you? What are you doing?' People value their privacy, and I was always trying to find out who they were and what they did for a living." But the problem eventually was solved. "Ultimately, I got a good job. What happened there was that my mom and dad were friends with Ted Dandurand [Sully's future father-in-law] who was Shirley's dad. Ted ran the meat market in town, and they got me a job in his meat market as a sort of general helper. Whatever. Clean up the place, do this and do that. Well, I kept that job mostly because Ted promised my parents not to fire me."

Shirley Marie Dandurand was born on August 26, 1939, in Marshall. She was just shy of two-and-a-half years younger than her future husband, Bob Sullivan. She grew up to become lovely in face and form with large, dark, dancing eyes as perhaps her most notable and attractive feature. "She was Catholic, but I never knew her for some reason. I never met her. So, I'm working for Ted's in the downstairs space and I'm sweeping up one day. And this gal comes down the stairs. The family lived upstairs, above the meat market. She comes walking down the stairs. I'll never forget it. She was in a navy-blue sweatshirt and light tan ranch pants. And this is the honest to God truth: I saw her, and I said, 'There's the girl I'm going to marry.' Without ever exchanging a word, I knew that. I knew who she was. I knew she was Ted's daughter. And she gets down there and looks at me and doesn't say anything. She puts the dustpan down and helps me while I'm sweeping up. And that started it. She'd come down and help me off and on." With the help of a broom and a dustpan, a budding romance blossomed. Bob and Shirley were an item from that point forward.

Bob and his teammates from Redeemer competed in athletics against kids from other Catholic schools as well as the public schools in the area until ninth grade, when he became a freshman at Central Catholic High School in 1952 The school was brand new as of 1950 and was part of a regional Catholic League of similarly situated schools. At the time there were eight regions statewide, each typically containing five or six teams, for a total of 40-plus Catholic schools throughout Minnesota. These teams were not associated with the State High School League and competed only among themselves. Some of the schools in Central's south/southwest region – Region 8 - included New Ulm Cathedral, Iona St. Columba, Sleepy Eye St. Mary's, and St. Adrian in Adrian (Sully still remembers Adrian seven decades later as having the prettiest cheerleaders.)

Central Catholic only stayed in operation for 17 years, closing its doors as a high school in 1967. The controlling Archdiocese decided at the time to close many of the schools in the Catholic system based on enrollment and other factors, including Central Catholic. The school still stands today as a grade school and according to Sully, the building and grounds look virtually the same as they did in the 1950s.

Central Catholic's athletic teams were called the Queensmen. An internet search of this term reveals, among other definitions (some not fit to print) that, "The Queen's Men were an acting company founded in 1583 by the Master of the Revels and Secretary of State Walsingham. The company was responsible for providing entertainment at the court during the Elizabethan era…" Why Central's school administrators and/or board members would choose this particular name is probably a mystery lost to history. Who are we to question? By golly, they were the Queensmen, and damn proud of it.

Bob made the basketball varsity as a freshman. One of his many claims to fame: "I think I am right about this when I say that I am the only basketball player to ever be named to the All-Region team all four years. The record will never be broken because the league doesn't exist anymore." He was also a basketball captain. Bob continued to play baseball and lettered three times in football as the team's quarterback. He also added track and field to his athletic resume. He competed in several events including the high jump, the long jump, and the sprints even though he was only "the third fastest guy on the team." He made the grave error once of finishing fifth in the Catholic state meet in the 880. Despite his fine performance, when he was done, he told his coach, "I don't ever want to run more than 100 yards again in my life."

Bob's coach throughout his career at Central in every single one of these sports was Tom Warner. "Tom was our coach for everything. He coached every sport that we had at Central. Plus he taught whatever he taught. He went on the become a great coach at Cretin." Indeed, after his career at Central, Warner served as both the head football and baseball coach at Cretin-Derham Hall High School in St. Paul from 1956-1966. He was inducted in CDH's Athletic Hall of Fame in 2024.

Bob remembered this man who was his first significant influence, mentor and role model in athletics: "He was a very good coach. He was really tough, in fact. I think, and my folks would probably tell you this too, he made a man of me. Literally. I mean, I was probably not very tough or whatever words you want to use. I loved the game and all that, but he really made you toe the mark. He was a disciplinarian for sure but, on the other hand, he encouraged you. He really knew the game. Great football and baseball coach, he didn't know basketball as well, so he just turned us loose to play. But he was a tough dude. He and Gagliardi, obviously, were my mentors." (More on the great John Gagliardi in the next chapter).

Bob excelled as a student at both Holy Redeemer and Central Catholic High but not because of any particularly arduous study schedule. "I was always a good student, naturally. For whatever reason, I never took a book home in high school. Never. But I made the top 10 in my class academically. And had good ACT scores and all that. But I never learned to study until I got to college… I had a great memory and was a great test taker. I loved taking tests. Yeah, most people don't, but I loved taking tests. So, I was just lucky I guess."

Bob was also an avid reader and has retained a love of books throughout his lifetime. "I was always a reader, I liked English, I later majored in English. I read a lot of books, mostly fiction; I was fascinated by Robert Louis Stevenson's stuff and even as a little kid by stories like *Snow White and the Seven Dwarfs*. My parents were not readers, there weren't many books in the house, so I guess I just came by it. Maybe it was the nuns, I don't know. Maybe they forced me to do it, I don't remember, but I didn't mind because I loved to read."

When it came time to choose a college Bob thought that St. Johns would be a good option. He wanted to continue to play basketball. "I sure as hell didn't look at St. Thomas, I knew that from day one. I had several buddies, including a guy named Nick Stevens, who went to St. Johns. A lot of the great athletes from Marshall that I had worshipped when I was young chose St. Johns. Really, anybody in our whole league, if he was any good, showed up there. So, I ended up at St. Johns, with everybody else." It was official: as of the fall of 1955, Bob Sullivan would be a Johnny.

CHAPTER 3

Gags & the St. John's University Johnnies

"We tell our football team that we don't have goals. Just do it, every day. I had that phrase long before Nike. Except I said it a little differently. I used to say, 'Just do it, goddammit.'"

JOHN GAGLIARDI

John Gagliardi hated the nickname "Gags." He never corrected anyone, for the simple reason that he didn't think it mattered much. If someone called him "Coach," he also did nothing other than assume the person did not know him very well. To his players he was always just "John," and he spent his entire life, and especially his professional career as a head football coach, striving mightily to stay focused only on what truly mattered: creating an atmosphere of high expectations; pursuing excellence in all things every single day; and, living by the golden rule that says, in his words, "Treat people how you would like to be treated, and that takes care of almost everything."

John Gagliardi (pronounced Gah-LAR-dee) was born in Trinidad, Colorado, on November 1, 1926. Like Bob Sullivan, he grew up a sports and especially football-loving kid. In 1943, when he was 16 and going into his senior year, his head football coach at Trinidad Catholic High School was called away to serve in World War II. School administrators decided to cancel the season, but Gagliardi approached the principal, Father Sebastiani, and asked for a reprieve. Gagliardi said, "Father, how about if we run practice ourselves? Just give us a week. If it's not working, you can always call it off." The reprieve was granted, and an epic coaching career began.

In his book, *The Sweet Season: A Sportswriter Rediscovers Football, Family, and a Bit of Faith at Minnesota's St. John's University,* author Austin Murphy relates what happened next: "Playing halfback in Trinidad's triple-threat offense and acting as coach, Gagliardi learned that many of football's hoariest traditions were superfluous – even downright stupid. The team stopped hitting five days a week. When the players got thirsty – here was a radical departure – they *drank water*. 'Hell, we figured they let horses drink water,' he says. The one thing that this newly minted player-coach most enjoyed about that season was that it included no calisthenics." The previous coach, like so many traditionalists of that era, took a hard-nosed, militaristic approach to football, which included calisthenics to the point of exhaustion. Murphy continues: "Trinidad won the first league championship in school history, proving what the adolescent Gagliardi had suspected: that jumping jacks, leg lifts, duckwalks and their idiotic ilk had as much to do with football as torture has to do with religion." Additionally, because the team that he coached consisted exclusively of his peer high school students, how could he ask them to call him anything other than John?

Gagliardi pursued his degree at Colorado College and continued to coach football at St. Mary's High School in Colorado Springs. Upon graduation, again like Bob Sullivan, he embarked on a career journey in the only job he would ever know: football coach. At age 22, not exactly wet behind the ears but still just a kid, Gags became the head football coach at Carroll College in Helena, Montana. He brought with him his iconoclastic philosophy and unique approach to the game. Over four seasons at Carroll, he compiled a 24-6-1 record to go with three Montana Collegiate Conference titles.

Saint John's University was chartered in 1857 by Benedictine monks who originally hailed from Pennsylvania. They had come west to provide spiritual leadership for the many Catholic immigrants who had chosen to settle in Stearns County, smack dab in the middle of the great state of Minnesota. Over the years, the institution became noted for training men of the cloth and came to be called the "Priest Factory." As sports entered the curriculum in a big way, St. John's joined the Minnesota Intercollegiate Athletic Association (MIAC) in 1920, as one of the conference's original charter members. The other original members were Carleton College, Gustavus Adolphus College, Hamline University, Macalester College, St. Olaf College, and the College of St. Thomas (all these schools except for St. Thomas are still members of the MIAC, more than a century later.)

In 1953, St. John's needed a new head football coach. The departing coach, John McNally, was a former Johnny who had starred at running back for the early teams in the 1920s. He went on to a fabulous, Hall-of-Fame career in the NFL, playing 14 seasons for several different teams and going by the unforgettable moniker of Johnny Blood. He was a likeable fellow and a great storyteller. As it turned out, Johnny Blood was a good guy and a hell of a player, but not as adept as a coach. From 1950-1952, he had the team firmly mired in what the monks considered to be unacceptable mediocrity, with an overall record of 13-9. The monks especially hated losing to the Lutherans at Gustavus and St. Olaf, and therefore they demanded better.

Twenty-six-year-old John Gagliardi interviewed for the position and no doubt impressed, for he was hired. When he asked Coach McNally why he was leaving, Johnny Blood lamented, "These Benedictines, they want to win, but they won't give you a nickel." As far as Gags was concerned, when the monks almost doubled his salary from $2,400 per year at Carroll to $4,400 in his new job, money was no issue at all. Austin Murphy describes well how

Gagliardi continued in his heretical ways: "In an era of screaming troglodytes who routinely abused their charges, verbally and physically; at a time when denying players water during practice and having them beat each other into steak tartar five times a week was seen not as sadism or idiocy but as *instilling toughness*, Gagliardi had the intelligence and courage to go in the other direction. You've heard of the uncola. Here was the uncoach, eschewing whistles, playbooks, blocking sleds, and agility drills. We've got limited time to work, Gags reasoned, so *let's practice the plays...* Gagliardi's focus has always been on preparation, execution, and fun."

Gags worked hard to make practice fun, and succeeded because he was tremendously funny, in a dry, understated, quirky way. In lieu of the dreaded calisthenics, the Johnnies would gather as a team and do such exercises as, "Deep Breath with Cheerleader Exhale." They all took a deep collective inhale, let it out, and then jumped around crazily, screaming wildly like, well, cheerleaders. They would do a partial jumping jack: no jump, just a hand clap. "Ear Warmups" consisted of taking the earlobe between thumb and forefinger and stretching it backward, forward, and sideways. In the "Nice Day" drill, they would all lay down on the ground, look up at the big blue sky and say to each other, "Nice day, isn't it?"

The seniors would lead the exercises, and every senior was a captain: "I want them to be able to put that on their resume." Hazing of freshmen was prohibited; every player was important; Gags required his seniors to seek out freshmen and sit with them in the dining hall. He refused to cut anybody; he couldn't bear the pain of that and so everyone made the team; some years the Johnnies had as many as 160 players or more on their roster.

Gagliardi was known to move practice inside when there was too much dew on the ground; he hated injuries, and someone might slip on the wet surface. When three players were hurt in succession in the last half hour of practice, Gags took the very logical step of cancelling the last half hour of practice going forward. Gnats drove him crazy. He once got a gnat embedded in his ear. The team watched dumbfounded, incredulous and then amused, as he walked to his car, turned on the headlights, and then stuck his ear right there in hopes the gnat would be attracted to the light. Out of that traumatic experience, on several occasions, he took the team indoors because of gnats.

There was virtually no contact in practice; everyone was off limits, not just quarterbacks. He reasoned, "What about those other guys? Hell, they've got mothers too." Instead of smashing into each other, he encouraged his players to "visualize" doing it. "Fantasies don't always have to be about the opposite sex," he told them.

Knowledgeable football people would surely say that any coach who promoted such asinine contrariness and rampant tomfoolery could not possibly field a competitive program. But along with the fun, Gagliardi unceasingly demanded that his players perform their jobs to the highest level of competence. In his book, *A Legacy Unrivaled: The Story of John Gagliardi*, author Boz Bostrom - who was an offensive lineman for Gags in the 1990s - explains, "John had high expectations of himself. He wouldn't just compare his success to that of other Division III coaches; rather, he would compare his win percentage to those of all-time greats like Bear Bryant, Woody Hayes, and Tom Osborne... It was the same thing on the football field: he had high expectations for his players and wanted them to have high expectations for their own performance." Repetition, proper execution, and accepting nothing less than excellence ensured that outcome. For John Gagliardi, four national titles and 489 career wins, the most in college football history, proved the point.

Bob Sullivan came to St. John's in the fall of 1955 with aspirations of making the varsity basketball team. He tried out but, lo and behold, "I found out I couldn't jump." It would be intramural hoops from there on out, with a bunch of his chums who had also been cut, and his team won a couple of school championships. He did not try out for football in his freshman season, but he found himself hanging around the program, taking in practices, following the team closely. He also took a class from a young instructor - who happened to be the head football coach - named John Gagliardi. The class was called, "Theory of Coaching Football."

In his sophomore year, Sully decided to try out for the football team. He remembered the moment well: "It was the beginning of spring practice. I lined up with everyone else to get football gear at the gym or wherever the hell it was. And Gagliardi sees me in there. He knew me because I had taken a class from him and hung around football all the time anyway. And he said, 'What are you doing?' I said, 'I'm going out for football.' He says, 'You're going to get killed out there.'" In those days players were expected to play both ways. Sully tipped the scale at about a buck forty and had never played defense in his life. Sully asked, "What do you mean?" Gagliardi reiterated: "You're going to get killed." Sully argued, "Listen, I can throw the ball better than anybody you got." Gags responded, "You hang around all the time anyway. Why don't you come coach with me?" Sully thought for just a moment, but what a pivotal moment it was: "Oh, well, okay." Another epic coaching career was launched.

Among the many parallels and commonalities in the lives and careers of Coach Gagliardi and Coach Sullivan is the fact that they were both married during this time. Gags married his sweetheart, Peggy Dougherty, on Valentine's Day, 1956. Sully wed his beloved Shirley Dandurand on the day after Christmas in 1957. Throughout their lives they were both devoted and loving husbands to their wives and fathers to their daughters (and sons too – each man had two daughters and two sons). Both generally adored and respected all women. Boz Bostrom quotes Gags as marveling about people of the opposite gender: "I think women came from a galaxy far away, drug us out of our caves with that stupid apple, and made us what we are. They must be superior. They live longer, they are smarter, are better looking, have nicer smiles, they become mothers and their kids like them better than their dads." Sully would no doubt concur with this analysis.

When the Sullivans were first married, while Bob continued to attend college, Shirley took a job as an administrative assistant in the Stearns County Attorney's office. Eventually, the couple rented a small apartment in St. Cloud, where the Gagliardis also made their home. When the newlyweds moved to their new apartment, which was right across the street from St. Cloud State University, Shirley went to work as an admin for one of the University vice presidents. She walked out the front door in the morning and was at work in less than five minutes.

Prior to his marriage, as his football education kicked off, Bob had already become a fixture in the Gagliardi home as he and Gags spent countless hours breaking down film together. Before Sully took on the responsibility of coaching the Johnny freshman teams in 1957 and 1958, he received a thorough tutorial from Gags in the art and science of football. As Bostrum points out, "John's dedication to breaking down game films is legendary." Sully recalled, "I spent half the time at his house, breaking down film. Wow. That was what he did: film breakdown. I had gotten to know him well by then. He was astute beyond belief, and I picked up on that and did the same thing. For the most part I just sat there and listened. I was so young. I asked him a question here and there, but I sure didn't try to tell him anything… He taught me how to watch film, for sure, and lots of it."

Sully also learned from Gagliardi's openness to new ways of thinking about football: "Oh, he was very liberal about that. He would pick up new ideas from a lot of great coaches and he would innovate. He started with the triple option before anybody in the league did it. And later he gravitated to the passing game, he picked up on that right away and went with it. He was very open football-wise to all the new things that came into the game. Because he studied the game totally, just like I did. He was never stuck on one thing; he was open to all that new stuff." Bostrum emphasizes the point: "Change does not scare John; rather, it energizes him." Gag's son, Johnny, who played at St. John's from 1977-1980 said about his father, "He really changed with the times. In the 1960s, he focused on the 'read' defense along with a power running game. In the 1970s, it was the quadruple option, in the 1980s, he started developing the passing game, and by the 1990s, he really opened up the passing game with an explosive, spread offense. He just kept getting better as the years went on."

In an era when many football coaches were big, burly men, all former college players themselves, some of them former military, who were prone to shouting, cursing and intimidating their players, neither John Gagliardi nor Bob

Sullivan even remotely fit the bill. Neither man was physically imposing. Neither had played college football. Both spoke with soft, calm voices that they rarely, if ever, raised. They were each more professorial in bearing and manner than rough and ready. They were both smart as hell and off the charts in football IQ. They were devoted students of their profession. They were both teachers first and took pride in that fact. Finally, they both understood the importance of adhering to the golden rule, which meant treating everyone, most especially the young men in their charge, with respect.

Gagliardi, in particular, reveled in presenting a somewhat disheveled, disorganized, can't maintain a train of thought persona. He occasionally said crazy shit. Some who did not know him well perhaps questioned his intelligence. In fact, he possessed a terrifically keen mind. "He is dumb as a fox," said Austin Murphy, after getting to know Gags well. Boz Boström said of his old coach, "One thing is his ability to deflect. He is the smartest guy I have ever met, sly like a fox." Bob Sullivan made this comparison: "The best way I can think of to describe him is that he was like Columbo. Remember Columbo? [*Columbo* was a popular television crime drama that ran for a decade in the '70s; the gifted actor Peter Falk starred as Lt. Columbo of the L.A.P.D., who was by all appearances completely out of his league; he was unkempt, unsophisticated, with a cigar hanging out of his mouth, and always driving murder suspects crazy with 'just one more question'; but he always outsmarted the bad guys and solved the crime in the end.] That was him. That was Gagliardi."

Bob Sullivan made his coaching debut in 1957 when Gags assigned him to lead the Johnny freshmen. During this period, Sully also served as the Sports Information Director for the college. He was entirely immersed in the world of athletics at St. Johns. In those days, no matter how talented they might be, freshmen could not play on the varsity. Therefore, Bob's clear mandate was to get those youngsters ready to step up and contribute at the varsity level by their sophomore year. He ran the same offense and defense as the varsity, with a focus on the power running game – three yards and a cloud of dust - and the 'read' defense, where the D-line is tasked with neutralizing the opposing offensive line, so that linebackers can read the play and make the tackle. Among other freshmen opponents in the 1957 and '58 seasons, the Johnnies played Carleton and St. Olaf. They played six games over two years. Gags never looked over Sully's shoulder; he let him loose to coach. Sully does not recall losing. He had done his job well, he loved teaching and coaching, and he was on his way, thanks to John Gagliardi.

John Gagliardi won 465 games in 60 seasons at St. Johns to go with his 24 wins at Carroll College. He won National Association of Intercollegiate Athletics national titles in 1963 and 1965. He won the Division III Natty in 1976 and 2003. He was the NAIA Coch of the Year in '65 and the American Football Coaches Association COY in 2003. He received the Amos Alonzo Stagg Award in 2009 for outstanding contributions to the game of football. He won 27 MIAC titles and was the MIAC COY nine times. He coached 113 All-Americas. Since 1993, the Gagliardi Trophy has gone to the outstanding player in Division III football. In 2006, he became the first active coach ever inducted into the College Football Hall of Fame.

John passed away, at the age of 91, after a long life well-lived, in October of 2018. The impact of his legacy on so many people is immeasurable.

At the end of his long, distinguished and decorated coaching career, John Gagliardi took time to write down his thoughts on how to measure success: "The work of any successful coach or teacher cannot – and should not – be viewed solely by whether, at season's end, his or her team has earned the label of champion. Rather, a coach's success can only accurately be measured years later – after the lessons, values and principles they instilled in their players have had the chance to manifest themselves in the form of their players becoming better parents, spouses, community leaders, teachers and, perhaps even, coaches. Only then, in the dim hindsight of time, can we truly judge how successful a coach has been."

CHAPTER 4

PREP DAYS

The Hill Pioneers & Cooper Hawks

"To me, being perfect is not about that scoreboard out there. It's not about winning. It's about you and your relationship to yourself and your family and your friends. Being perfect is about being able to look your friends in the eye and know that you didn't let them down, because you told them the truth. And that truth is that you did everything that you could... Can you live in that moment, as best you can, with clear eyes and love in your heart? If you can do that gentlemen, then you're perfect. I want you to take a moment. And I want you to look each other in the eyes. I want you to put each other in your hearts forever, because forever is about to happen here in just a few minutes..."

FROM THE HALFTIME SPEECH BY PERMIAN HIGH, ODESSA TEXAS COACH GARY GAINES (PORTRAYED BY ACTOR BILLY BOB THORNTON) IN THE MOVIE FRIDAY NIGHT LIGHTS

Bob Sullivan was a good, but not great student at St. John's. "I was not an 'A' student. I was a 'B' student, I think about a 3.1 or something like that. Problem was when I got there, I didn't know how to study. I had been a top ten student at Central Catholic without ever bringing a book home. I had a photographic memory [while science disputes that there is such a thing as a true 'photographic memory,' in Sully's case there is no doubt that his recall, particularly for details from his football career and about his players, is utterly phenomenal] and that got me through. I was a great test taker. But when I got to St. Johns, I ran into a kid I knew from Cretin High School. His name was Peter Powell. I had a picture of Shirley on the desk in my dorm room, and he would admire that picture. Peter and I had two classes together and one day he said, 'Let's go study.' I said, 'Go study? What do you mean go study?' But that's what we did, and he taught me how to study, this kid." When asked whether Peter taught him how to study, or just that he had to study, Sully responded, "Both."

With a new outlook and commitment to academics, Sully got through the coursework in his English major, graduating also with a minor in physical education. He knew he wanted to coach and teach English. Thanks to help from Tom Warner and John Gagliardi, opportunity came knocking right away.

The Institute of the Brothers of the Christian Schools is a Catholic lay religious congregation dedicated to education. Its founder was Jean-Baptiste de La Salle, a French priest and educational reformer who lived from 1651 to 1719. The Christian Brothers established Hill High School in 1959 as a school for young men. In 1971, Hill High consolidated with Archbishop Murray Memorial High School to form Hill-Murray. Murray had been started in 1958 by the Benedictine Sisters as a school for young women.

The school is part of the Roman Catholic Archdiocese of St. Paul and Minneapolis and continues to thrive today on a 40-acre campus located in Maplewood, Minnesota. Hill-Murray is known for a great sports tradition and has been especially dominant in recent decades with multiple Minnesota

State High School League hockey championships. But in 1959 the operation was entirely brand new, and the administration urgently sought capable teachers and coaches.

Sully recalled, "Tom Warner was then the coach at Cretin, and he wanted me to come onto his staff as an assistant. But he also told me about the opportunity at Hill. Of course, the head coaching role was the one I wanted to pursue. But it was thanks to Tom, and with a recommendation from Gagliardi too, that I got the job at Hill."

Hill began its operations as an all-boys school with just freshmen and sophomores enrolled. "I suppose it was for economic reasons, and at that time St. Thomas Academy and Cretin were the big powerhouses in St. Paul. Probably some upperclassmen from STA and Cretin just did not want to attend the new school. But the basic idea was to start with underclassmen and build up from there. So technically, we did not have our first full varsity season with juniors and seniors until 1961. We ran a freshman team and a B squad with sophomores in the first year, then the next year we actually played three varsity games, and then five other JV games."

Hill was in the Central Catholic Conference (CCC), arguably the second most competitive league in the state at the time, behind only the Lake Conference, which was comprised of large Twin Cities area high schools. The Pioneers played an eight-game schedule and competed against such schools as St. Thomas Academy, Cretin, DeLaSalle, Rochester Lourdes, and Winona Cotter.

At that time, Sully recalled, there were more than 30 Catholic high schools playing football in Minnesota. None of these schools, including the eight in the CCC, were technically part of the Minnesota State High School League. The Catholic conferences operated by their own rules.

As a result, Coach was permitted to recruit, which he proceeded to do with energy from his inaugural season. "I would go to grade school basketball games, identify the best athletes, and try to recruit them to Hill. The Christian Brothers who ran the school, who were out of Chicago, were used to this; they wanted to win in sports, so they actually helped kids financially to come to our school. We even recruited at places like White Bear Lake. The public schools didn't like us much, because we would pick off some of their best kids."

Sully considered himself a defensive specialist in the first several years of his career, but he gradually gravitated to the offensive side of the ball. "As a former quarterback, I was drawn to the concept of throwing the football. I always leaned toward the passing game. At Hill we ran most of the time, as much as 80 percent, but we threw it occasionally too. We ran the twin veer of course but also featured multiple formations and motion. The defense was a 52 read [five down linemen and two linebackers in the box; see Chapter 9], also a Gagliardi scheme, which I used all the way to Carleton."

"We had good athletes from the very beginning," said Sully. "The freshman team was undefeated that first year." Coach remembered the very first game in the full varsity season of '61. "We were playing Mahtomedi, and they were on a 25-game win streak and were favored, big. We beat 'em, 7-0, at Mahtomedi. I'll never forget the headline the next day: 'Hill High School, New Football Power.'"

In that first season, Hill went 4-4-1. Six of Sully's guys were first-team All-CCC. He had the athletes, and things would improve in the coming campaigns. In 1962, the Pioneers were 5-4, losing close games to DeLaSalle and St. Thomas. The school yearbook commented that, "The Pioneers crushing win over Central and hard-fought loss to Cretin [28-20] were truly memorable games." The next year, 1963, they achieved another 5-4 season, but the team lost by only one point to mighty Cretin. They were making progress, and 1964 would be a breakthrough season.

The Catholic Bulletin of the Archdiocese of St. Paul, established by Archbishop John Ireland in 1911, was a concise weekly newspaper that, among other things, reported on sports in the Catholic high school leagues around the state. Each year, the Bulletin identified the top football team in the state, and the Pioneers won the honor in '64. The school yearbook proclaimed: "The final score: Hill 198, Opponents 63. This score tells the story of Hill's football campaign... as the Pioneers rolled up a 7-1 record. On the 'Catholic Bulletin' ratings we were acclaimed State Champions."

Hill went 6-2 in 1965, and again won the state title in '66, despite an unremarkable 5-3 record. The Pioneers lost two non-conference games but went 4-1 in the CCC, to win a share of the title. Among other highlights, Hill finally defeated Cretin for the first time. Once again, the Catholic Bulletin identified Hill as the best of the Catholic teams in the state. They were 7-2 in both 1967 and '68. In 1969, the Pioneers stumbled to a disappointing 3-6 finish, Sully's only losing season at Hill.

Sully did have an abundance of outstanding athletes from the very beginning. He fondly reminisced about some of his star players: "Tom Kinsella, who was there when I got there, was a standout that I remember. He went to the University of Minnesota where he backed up Bobby Bell as a defensive tackle. Another great defender was Jack Reif, who was a high school All-America at linebacker for me. He also went on the play at the U of M. Rick Cover was a transfer from Mississippi, believe it or not, came to us in his junior year, who was our all-everything running back. He held all our rushing records at the time. He went to NDSU where he played free safety and won consecutive national championships. John Goebel was also a terrific running back for us in the mid-'60s. He went to St. Thomas where he led them in rushing for several years. He also went with the Vikings in the year that there was a strike [the NFLPA voted to strike briefly in 1968.] He stuck with them for a while but got cut eventually. But he was great back, a helluva player. I'll bet we sent four or five kids every year to college football."

Two fellow St. John's alums were incredibly valuable to Sully at Hill as assistant coaches. Like Sully, Roger Ludwig was a 1959 Johnny grad who was talented enough as a football player to receive a tryout with the Minnesota Vikings (he did not make the team.) Ludwig was the defensive coordinator at Hill and, Sully said, "had a heart of gold." Bob Stolz was a 1960 St. John's grad who was All-Conference as an offensive tackle. In addition to serving as Sully's very competent offensive line coach, Stolz taught science at Hill.

Coach Sullivan did an outstanding job at Hill. He had an overall record of 49-28-1, with an excellent winning percentage of .628. He never had a losing season except for his last one in 1969. And he and his Pioneers experienced the triumph of capturing Catholic state titles in 1964 and 1966. But by 1969, Coach was ready for a change.

All four of the Sullivan children were born during Bob's time at Hill. The first-born, Anastasia (Stacy) Marie, came along in February of 1961; Timothy Emmet was born in April 1962; Bob (Bubba) Theodore in June of 1966; and Molly Lynn in July 1969 (more on the Sullivan family in Chapter 18). Of course, Bob and Shirley both very much wanted to have a family, but there was an added benefit: for each child, Sully received an additional $100 in monthly salary. On a high school coach's income, that was good money. So, procreation made both emotional and financial sense. Many years later, Bubba said to his father with a smile, "Gee Dad, I'm so glad I was worth a hundred bucks to you."

Edwin J. Cooper was the popular superintendent of the Robbinsdale Area School District #281. In 1964, E.J. Cooper Senior High School, named in his honor, opened its doors for the first time. The school had been established in response to a growing student population in the district. In the beginning, Cooper was comprised of kindergarten and grades 10, 11 and 12. The ninth grade was added in the 1990s. What is now known as Robbinsdale Cooper High School continues to prosper today, with a student population of 1,600, on its campus in New Hope, just northwest of the City of Minneapolis.

When Bob Sullivan arrived as the new head football coach in the fall of 1970, the school was only in its seventh year of operation and its football program was in tough shape. They had won only nine games in six years. The district had recently split into three high schools: Cooper, Robbinsdale and Armstrong. Several key players for Cooper enrolled at Armstrong, leaving Coach Sullivan with only one starter from the previous year.

Sully had wanted this job and considered the transition from the CCC to the more prestigious and competitive Lake Conference a good career move. He received an annual salary increase, going from somewhere around $12-13,000 in his last year at Hill to $19-20,000 at Cooper (Coach was never in it for the money; he is fuzzy in his recollection of salary figures throughout his career; don't ask what his starting salary was at Carleton because he doesn't remember.)

Nevertheless, there were substantial obstacles from the beginning. "It was a step up, but when I got there, I realized the vast cultural difference between a private and a public school." The still youthful 33-year-old coach would be supremely challenged in his first true turnaround effort to build a winning tradition. "It was the toughest job I ever had."

The 1970 Cooper Hawks posted a record of 0-7-1. They tied Minnetonka, and in the most exciting game of the season almost defeated the formidable Hornets of Edina. Cooper scored at the very end of regulation to bring them within one point of the Hornets. Rather than kick the extra point for the tie, Sully manned up and went for two and the win. Their pass attempt failed, was knocked away in the end zone, and Edina prevailed 23-22.

Edina was coached by the legendary Stavros Canakes, one of Minnesota's all-time greats (the author played for Stav Canakes at Edina West just a few years later; more in Chapter 19), who approached Sully after the game and expressed relief for the win and congratulations for the valiant effort. But the loss still stung. All the losses hurt. He never got used to losing. Coach knew this would be a long hard road and a multi-year turnaround.

The next two years brought two wins in each season. Finally, in 1973, the tide began to turn a bit, and there were three four-win seasons in the next four years. In 1976, the team won three of their final four games, a hugely positive omen leading up to the 1977 campaign. By this time, Coach had higher numbers participating, better athleticism, and smarter players. "In my first several seasons, I didn't have a single kid in the National Honor Society. In 1977 and '78, I had at least seven or eight in the Honor Society. I also had at least seven or eight who went on to play college football."

Sully remembered some of his best athletes from those two teams: "Steve Ferry was an All-State player. We converted him from a tight end to running back and he was terrific. He played in the State All-Star game at season's end. He went on to St. John's and had a great career there." Ferry was a fine all-around athlete who, in addition to captaining the football and hockey teams, also played baseball. He was an All-Conference tight end in 1976 who set Cooper season records for receptions, yardage and scoring. He moved to running back in '77 and did just as well, being named All-Conference with 630 rushing yards, 163 receiving yards, and seven touchdowns, to go with three interceptions on defense.

"'Bomber' Johnson was a tight end and defensive end for us. He went on first to junior college and then to star at Iowa State. He played for the Miami Dolphins in the NFL. In the only Super Bowl that Dan Marino ever quarterbacked in, Bomber caught a TD pass from him." When asked what Bomber's true first name was, Sully took a guess: "Dan?" He was correct. Dan Johnson was picked in the seventh round of the 1983 draft by the Dolphins and played seven NFL seasons. He had 94 career receptions and 16 career touchdowns, including catching the only touchdown pass that Hall of Fame quarterback Dan Marino threw in a losing effort in Super Bowl XIX.

"Bruce Harmon was also a receiver, and when he graduated, he went to South Dakota State. He was a really fast kid, and a bit of a showboat. He was the kind who when he scored, he would strike the 'Heisman' pose. You know? That kind of kid. But a helluva player." Harmon set four Cooper individual receiving records in 1978: most receiving yards in a season with 643; most receiving yards in a game with 158; most receptions in a season with 41; and he tied several others for most receptions in a game with seven. Harmon went on to set records at South Dakota State.

Two assistant coaches who were critical to the ultimate success of the program at Cooper were Bob Lorentzen and Jim Knight. Lorentzen coached the offensive line. He had been a defensive end at Mankato State and was the father of star quarterback Jim Lorentzen. In his collegiate days, Knight was an All-Conference quarterback at Gustavus and at Cooper he served ably as Sully's defensive coordinator.

The 1977 team broke the Cooper record of four wins in a season handily, to post an 8-1 record and win a share of the Lake Conference Red Division title. There were 17 returning lettermen and 22 seniors on the squad. Cooper was ranked number one in the state early on but then lost to Richfield late in the season. Coach Sullivan was named the Region 6AA Coach of the Year by his peers for leading Cooper to the first winning record in its 14-year history.

The 1978 team was also 8-1, missing out on a perfect season with a heartbreaking final game loss to Fridley. The offensive attack was explosive, with quarterback Jim Lorentzen breaking the school's record for total offense in a season with 1,248 yards passing and 1,395 total yards. He threw 14 touchdown passes, also a record. Senior co-captain Jim Tabor led the team in rushing, with a school record of 838 yards. The Lake Conference had renamed its two divisions, from Red and Blue to North and South. In 1978, the Hawks again won a share of the conference divisional title, this time the Lake Conference North.

Tim Sullivan was a backup quarterback for his dad in '77 and'78. He tells the story of a cold, rainy day as the team prepared to head out to practice. Sully always declared, "It never rains on Cooper football." The guys rolled their eyes and anticipated the worst as they left the locker room. Sully led the charge, and the moment he ran outside, the rain suddenly stopped. When asked whether, based on this apparent meteorological miracle, the players assumed that their coach had some kind of other-worldly powers, Tim responded, "Well, we didn't assume he had special powers, but he sure did."

In both 1977 and '78, talented and worthy though they were, Cooper lost out on the opportunity to go on to the state playoffs because of a convoluted computer ranking system. The bottom line was that in both seasons, in order to break a tie between teams, the deciding factor became a tally of computer points. The Hawks fell just short.

Nevertheless, the team whose prospects had been so dismal when Coach Sullivan arrived in 1969 had won 20 of its last 23 games. Spirits were high, and the future looked bright for the fighting Cooper Hawks.

In 1978, decision makers in School District 281 determined that they needed to trim the budget. Sully's job as a coach and English teacher was in jeopardy. He was quoted at the time in the local sports page: "It looks like I'll be looking for something else soon. Like so many other schools, Cooper is cutting back. My nine years aren't enough to preserve my job." Later in his career, Coach commented that the cutbacks were not such a huge factor, "Maybe number five on my list of reasons to move on."

Sully was ready for a change. He had turned a football program around in dramatic fashion. He was anxious to move to the college ranks. He still aspired to become the head coach at Notre Dame. He was 41 years old, a young man but an ol' ball coach with 20 years of hard-won experience. He still had an exciting future in front of him. When he heard the news that Carleton College needed a new head football coach, he jumped at the chance. His life would never be the same.

Local sportswriter Greg Carlson penned an article on February 8, 1979, entitled "Sully Will Be Missed." He said, "Cooper High School lost a great coach when Bob Sullivan accepted the head football position at Carleton College last week. In nine years at Cooper, Sullivan accomplished what few coaches are capable of doing: he took a football program that was labeled a loser in the Lake Conference, suffered through seven campaigns without a winning record and finally produced two teams that tied for the division championship. More significantly along the way, Sullivan taught his players the importance of having a positive attitude, to set goals for themselves and to have pride in their school. These are lessons about life, not football."

In the same piece, Cooper principal Elmer Kemppainen praised Coach: "He always had a very positive attitude. It took a few years to get a winner, but it's a tribute to him that he didn't give up. Sully has been good, real good. We're going to miss him."

CHAPTER 5

RENAISSANCE MAN

Poetry & Music

"O my luve's like a red, red rose,
That's newly sprung in June:
O my luve's like a melodie
That's sweetly play'd in tune.
As fair art thou, my bonny lass,
So deep in luve am I;
And I will luve thee still, my dear,
Till a' the seas gang dry..."

ROBERT BURNS

Bob Sullivan has always been an inveterate reader, and among many other literary genres, he loves poetry. Over the years, he has tried his hand at writing his own poetry. Once, when he was a sophomore English major at St. John's, he had a poetic inspiration. As he was riding home in the back seat of a friend's car one evening, a poem came to him (the poem has since been lost to the dustbin of history.) "I conjured this poem in my head. It just came to me for whatever reason. I got back to the dorm and wrote it down. It was the best poem I had ever written to that point, and I submitted it for publication to a student-run literary publication on campus. One day a knock came on my door, and the editor-in-chief, a senior but still just a student like me, came into the room and accused me of plagiarism. His assumption was there was no way a jock like this guy Sullivan could compose such a fine poem. I pushed back hard and told him he was wrong. But they never did publish the poem." Sully tells the story with scorn and irritation that persists to this day. "Don't make assumptions about people is the lesson learned."

While he was at Cooper, Coach made the decision to pursue a masters degree in English at the University of Wisconsin-River Falls. It made sense on multiple levels. First, it was just something he wanted to do. He loved to learn, and this was a chance to do just that in a big way. He liked the idea of studying a topic completely unrelated to his primary passion, football. River Falls had a great program and was proximate to the Sullivan home in Mahtomedi, only about 30 miles away. Finally, just as he was rewarded financially for having children, his salary would also go up based on his owning a graduate degree. "I think it was another $200 per month, or something like that." To procreate and educate, therefore, became the goal.

He attended UW-River Falls for the equivalent of three terms, in the summer during the mid-1960s, and it took him two years to complete the degree. "I thoroughly enjoyed the program. I had great classes and wonderful professors. I took classes in English Literature, Shakespeare, the Romantic Poets, and World Literature. All excellent stuff." Sully particularly reveled in studying the lives and poetry of the great Romantic poets: William Wordsworth, Samual Taylor Coleridge, John Keats, Percy Shelley, Lord Byron, and William Blake, among others.

The Romantic intellectual movement originated in the late 1700s and lasted for perhaps half a century. It represented a farewell to old Neoclassical modes of thinking and a welcoming of new poetic styles that were spontaneous, imaginative, and sounded different. The Romantics focused on "sublime" experiences that went beyond the ordinary, and on humanity's relationship with the environment.

Sully's favorite poet was Robert Burns, who was among the early pioneers of the Romantic movement. Many scholars refer to Burns as a "pro-to-Romantic" poet, who greatly influenced the talented group of wordsmiths who came later. Burns was born in 1759 and died at age 37, but he did a great deal of living during that brief time span.

The idea of a national poet, someone who represents and exemplifies a nation's culture, emerged during the Romantic era. Burns is to this day widely considered the national poet of Scotland. He lacked formal education and was a failure as a farmer, but eventually caught on and began to make some money as a poet and lyricist. Burns composed in the Scots language, but much of his work was written in a dialect that was closer to English, thus making his poetry accessible to a wider audience. He was a charmer and serial womanizer who had love affairs with many women, several of whom bore him children. He wrote poetry to and about some of those women. Burns came of age during the American and French Revolutions, and he was a staunch advocate for democratic and parliamentary reform. His political views sometimes got him into trouble.

In his splendid book, *The Bard: Robert Burns: A Biography*, scholar and author Robert Crawford expanded on the characteristics that made Burns such an important literary figure: "No writer is more charismatic than Robert Burns. Passionate, intelligent, and a consummate wordsmith, he is the world's most popular love poet. He sought to become, and became, the archetypal national bard. Though it was dangerous to be so in his age and place, he also made himself through tone and temperament the master poet of democracy... Burns achieved his successes not with transcendental illumination but with daftness, deftness, warmth, humor, and a sometimes painful sense of his own vulnerability. No poet has been at once so brilliant and so down-to-earth."

Sully always relished researching the life and poetry of Robert Burns. What was the draw? "Well, he was really talented and had a fascinating life." Also, while Sully has always been a faithful husband, father and friend, there is no doubt that he, like Robert Burns, simply adores women. Was the fact that Burns was a "love poet" who was mesmerized by the opposite sex something that piqued Sully's interest? "Could be," was the answer. The proof probably lies in the title of Sully's master's thesis, the well-researched and written paper that earned him his graduate degree: *Robert Burns & His Wom-*

en (another treasured bit of scholarship that has been lost to posterity; Sully thinks there may be a copy in a box somewhere in his garage).

Another prevalent theme in Romantic poetry was melancholy. During periods of his life when he experienced loss or sadness, Sully was sometimes moved to assuage his own melancholy by writing poetry. In early 2011 he penned this poem:

TRUE TO US

"The sadness creeps over me
Like ocean waves lapping the shore
Knowing full well – while hoping against
They will someday cease.

The why's and what if's continue
Their turmoil, but your beauty
And devotion sustain me even now
In this all too uncertain turbulent terrain.

I want to praise, glorify repent
Thank and beg; all at the same time;
Knowing that I will never know
Yet continue to press the unintelligible
Limits of human feelings and love."

Like the Romantic poets, Sully also explored themes of nature. Here is a poem, also from 2011:

ANGRY WINDS

"The hot winds blow furiously through the trees
Making them seem angry and wild
Like life is in a state of upheaval
With no hope of normality
Who or what will it take to bring life and love into focus?
The trees wait for the winds to die.
Only time will heal the ripping and tearing of their limbs and leaves
Till then the eternal fight for survival continues
When the raging winds finally cease
Then there will be peace."

And of course, Bob Sullivan was a love poet:

LOVE HUNGER

"Do we have any idea how many people
Are looking for love and how lucky some
Are to have found it at all?

Despite the many definitions of love –
They are all <u>critically important at the time,</u>
<u>Regardless of social, religious or popular opinion.</u>
<u>That is what makes it so unique – love defies</u>
<u>Definition or universality – hail to love and romance –</u>
<u>One of God's greatest gifts to man.</u>

<u>I see all around me – constantly – love hunger and all</u>
<u>Of its personifications. God is there – non-judgmental</u>
Yet understanding and smiling, "I Love You No Matter What."

Do not waste your time on judgment or analysis,
Take advantage before the sun sets, it will
Not be by this way again".

Sully has loved music for all his life, but once he reached young adulthood, the genre of country western caught his fancy. One of his most famous "Sullyisms" was a prediction concerning his players: "You guys will all love country western music by the time you're 30." He came by his passion for this style of music on his own, just as he did his love of sports, but later in his life. He was exposed to classical music and other forms in his youth. His parents enjoyed music and dancing, but neither of them was a country fan. In the 1960s, Sully started by becoming seriously interested in folk music (Peter, Paul & Mary were special favorites, as were Woody and Arlo Guthrie) and he graduated to country from there.

Sully's all-time top country singer was Waylon Jennings, who was born just a few months after Sully in June of 1937, and passed away in 2002. Waylon fashioned himself as an outlaw and Sully liked that about him. Waylon teamed up with the rest of Sully's outlaw favorites, Willie Nelson (born in 1933), Kris Kristofferson (born in 1936 and died in 2024), and the great Johnny Cash (born in 1932 and died in 2003) to form a group called The Highwaymen, who put out several successful albums during the decade from 1985 to'95. Their best song, in Sully's opinion, was composed by Waylon and Willie and became a big hit for the Highwaymen: "Good Hearted Woman." From this older generation of country performers, Sully also reveled in the eloquent songwriting and gorgeous singing voice of Emmylou Harris.

From the next generation of singer/songwriters, Sully listens to Alan Jackson, Toby Keith, Travis Tritt, Roseann Cash (Johnny's daughter), and Pam Tillis. One of Alan Jackson's songs that particularly resonates with Sully is called, "The Older I Get." The first and final verses go as follows:

"The older I get
The more I think
You only get a minute, better live while you're in it
'Cause it's gone in a blink
And the older I get
The truer it is
It's the people you love, not the money and stuff
That makes you rich…

The older I get
The longer I pray
I don't know why, I guess that I've got more to say
And the older I get
The more thankful I feel
For the life I've had and all the life I'm living still"

Sully tells an incredibly bittersweet story about the country artist Toby Keith, who died of stomach cancer at age 62 in February of 2024. "Toby was riding in a golf cart several years ago at some event with the actor Clint Eastwood [who was born in 1930 and is still active in the movie business in Hollywood] when Clint was about as old as I am now, late 80s. Clint was making a new movie and Toby asked him, 'How do you keep doing it after all these years?' Clint said, 'I get up every day and go out, and I don't let the old man in.' Toby got inspired and wrote the song, 'Don't Let the Old Man In.'" Here are some verses from Toby Keith's beautiful lilting ballad:

"…And I knew all of my life
That someday it would end
Get up and go outside
Don't let the old man in

Many moons I have lived
My body's weathered and worn
Ask yourself how you would be

If you didn't know the day you were born

Try to love your wife
And stay close to your friends
Toast each sundown with wine
Don't' let the old man in…"

Sully said softly, "I love that song."

CHAPTER 6

FOOTBALL TEACHES LIFE

The Psychology of Winning

"The most important single point in the chapters to follow, to remember and internalize, is that it makes little difference what is actually happening, it's how you, personally, take it that really counts!"

FROM THE PSYCHOLOGY OF WINNING BY DENIS WAITLEY

Denis Waitley's philosophy around what he called the Psychology of Winning (POW) captured Bob Sullivan's imagination. Sometime in the mid-1970s, exact date unknown, Waitley spoke at a football clinic that Sully attended. Waitley was a nationally recognized authority on high-level performance and personal development. At the clinic, he explained his formula for developing the ten qualities of a "total winner." Sully followed up by listening to Waitley's best-selling and more in-depth audiocassette program. The Coach was sold. Forever afterward, POW served as a centerpiece in his approach to teaching his guys not only how to be good football players, but excellent young men too.

Denis Waitley was born in 1933, attended the U.S. Naval Academy, and served as a naval aviator. When he left the military, he worked in jobs in public relations and charitable fundraising before developing his hugely successful motivational program. He produced popular and lucrative audio courses and went on to write many books, the most notable of which was *The Psychology of Winning* (1979), which sold more than two million copies. He made a handsome living as a keynote speaker and consultant to high-level leaders in government and business.

Later in his career, Waitley suffered the embarrassment of forced resignation from a corporate board after revelations that he did not actually possess a master's degree, as he claimed, and that his doctoral degree, such as it was, came from an unaccredited institution. Woops. Sully didn't care. So the guy prevaricated; so what? Sully said, "Not too worried about that. His main idea is still important and relevant. It is that people need to take control of their lives, respond positively no matter what happens, and pursue excellence in all things. People who do those things are winners. Those are the key lessons I wanted my players to get from POW."

According to "Dr." Waitley, the ten qualities of a total winner are:

- **Positive Self-awareness:** "Winners know who they are, what they believe, the role in life that they are presently fulfilling, and their great personal potential."

- **Positive Self-esteem:** "Winners have a deep-down feeling of their own worth.… Recognizing their uniqueness, they develop and maintain their own high standards."

- **Positive Self-control:** "Winners 'make' it happen. Losers 'let' it happen.… Winners realize they personally have the power to take control of many more aspects of their lives, both mental and physical, than were heretofore thought possible."

- **Positive Self-motivation:** "Winners dwell on their desires, not their limitations.… With this in mind, they focus their thinking on the rewards of success and actively tune out fears of failure."

- **Positive Self-expectancy:** "Winners expect to win. They know that so-called 'luck' is the intersection of preparation and awareness."

- **Positive Self-image:** "Winners are especially aware of the tremendous importance of their self-image, and of the role their imagination can play in the creation and up-grading of the self-image."

- **Positive Self-direction:** "Winners in life have clearly defined, constantly referred to, game plans and purposes… Their objectives range all the way from daily priorities to lifetime goals."

- **Positive Self-discipline:** "Winners practice flawless techniques in their minds, over and over and again and again. They know that thought begets habit, and they discipline their thoughts to create the habit of superb performance."

- **Positive Self-dimension:** "Winners see their total person in such a fully-formed perspective that they literally become part of the 'big picture' of life – and it of them. They have learned how to know themselves intimately."

- **Positive Self-projection:** "Winners project an aura; they have an unmistakable presence; they have a charisma which is disarming, radiating and magnetic. They project that warm glow that comes from inside out."

Waitley concluded, "When you project the Ten Qualities of a Total Winner into your own life, they can become your own Ten Commandments for personal growth and achievement of your own individual definition of success."

For Coach Sullivan, the challenge became how to interpret and teach these arguably esoteric platitudes to a bunch of football players – who were skeptics too, especially at Carleton - in a way that would resonate and be helpful to them. He also needed to make the principles relevant to football.

Accordingly, Coach took Waitley's material and developed his own outline, with his unique take on the content, typed by the man himself in the days when people sat at a typewriter and typed. To emphasize its importance, he placed this outline at the beginning of the extensive playbook that each member of the team received to commence the season. When he stood up to address the boys for the first time, every year, starting at Cooper High and throughout his Carleton career, the Psychology of Winning was subject Number One on the agenda.

First, Sully emphasized the importance of optimism versus pessimism. You can control your attitude, and positivity beats negativity every time. An optimistic athlete is more likely to achieve optimal performance and, as a result, more likely to win. Coach even believed there was a connection between optimism and injury prevention; the football player who worries about getting hurt frequently does just that. Winners, Sully stated emphatically in his outline, "HAVE A POSITIVE EXPECTANCY OF WINNING BIG" (his emphasis).

Building on the importance of viewing things in a favorable light, Coach told his guys to see problems as opportunities. This approach was football relevant, for example, in what Sully called "sudden change" scenarios. The outcome of a game will often turn on events that quickly shift the fortunes of a team, such as a lost fumble, a pick six or a blocked kick. Sully said, "Find something good in every situation... Stay cool, fake it at first, if necessary, this skill will be learned." The best teams remain confident and calm under pressure; they welcome the do-or-die moment in any contest; they believe that they will prevail in just such moments.

Visualization was a key skill: "Don't be afraid to dream the 'Big Dream'... Sports are full of examples – the seven-foot high jump, the four-minute mile, the nine-flat one-hundred-yard dash, 1000-yard rushers. Football lends itself particularly to the 'big play' dream from week to week." Sully exhorted his guys to "Visualize the rewards of success, strength, speed, tackles, touchdowns, WINNING."

Persistence was critical. He quoted one of his favorite characters from history, Sir Winston Churchill, who amidst the throes of WWII, when the Brits were up against it, addressed the students at Harrow School, his alma mater. He told them, "Never give in. Never give in. Never, never, never, never – in nothing great or small, large or petty – never give in."

Sully ended the outline with a recitation of his own creed, based on his life's journey and observations about the human condition, in a section he called "Portrait of a Winner":

> *"They are highly organized toward the future with a positive expectancy.*
> *They tend to be warm, outgoing people.*
> *They tend to put themselves and others 'up' and not 'down.'*
> *If they criticize, they criticize the act and not the person.*
> *They don't spread bad news – rather they simply talk about events and issues.*
> *They have a highly defined conscience, and an acute sense of right and wrong.*
> *They are very trusting and have faith in their relationships.*
> *They are people of great accountability (they accept blame).*
> *They have fine leadership qualities.*
> *THEY HAVE A POSITIVE EXPECTANCY OF WINNING BIG."*

More than 40 years later, Brent Siegel, '83, who was a team captain in his senior season and enjoyed a long and successful career in sales, recalled the impact that the Psychology of Winning approach had on him: "Sully had a defined concept focused on positive thinking, football schemes, and having a winning mindset. His program was about more than football. He created a culture that showed me a new way of thinking about the team, the game and myself. He also approached the game intellectually, which allowed us to compete without having the biggest, strongest or fastest players. It was the first time I had ever thought about applying finesse and skill instead of brute force. One key was his use of metrics and goals for the team – those key indicators that if achieved would most often result in a win for Carleton. Finally, He also asked us to set goals for ourselves each week and write them down and give them to our position coach. Again, it was all about more than football; it was about life."

Jon Darby, also class of 1983, became a top official in the U.S. intelligence community, ending his career as one of the highest-ranking civilian executives in the National Security Agency. He recalled Sully's influence on his approach to leadership: "His impact has been immeasurable on my life and career. At work I have led teams as small as two and as large as tens of thousands. The best leadership training I ever had was playing team sports growing up, culminating in playing football and baseball at Carleton. On the football team, I had a front row seat in observing how Sully set the tone for the team with preparation, a positive attitude and care for all the players, and the value each one brought as an individual to the team. I tried to bring that same people-oriented, optimistic and outcome-oriented approach to my leadership over the ensuing decades."

Bob Mackin was a team captain in 1981 and is now a PhD and Associate Professor in the Medical College of Georgia Department of Cellular Biology and Anatomy. Sully demonstrated to him a new way of thinking about leadership and how to motivate people: "My high school football coach was the complete opposite of Bob Sullivan. His main motivating factor was fear of failure, and he set himself up as the bad cop while leaving the rest of the coaching staff to play the good cop. Having Bob Sullivan coach using a positive mindset was a dramatic revelation in how you can lead by positive motivation. As the parent of three children, I jumped at the chance to help coach their sports teams. I wanted to exemplify how positive coaching could be both successful in terms of wins and losses, and lead to an enhanced team sports experience for the players. So many parents want their children to participate in sports for the wrong reasons that I hoped the kids I coached came away from our season together having benefited as athletes, teammates and people."

CHAPTER 7

The Creation of a Game & the Carleton College Knights

"You young men will come to no Christian end!"

A RUTGERS PROFESSOR SHOUTING FROM THE SIDELINE DURING THE FIRST COLLEGE FOOTBALL GAME, BETWEEN RUTGERS AND PRINCETON, NOVEMBER 6, 1869

If you have ever watched little boys play together it becomes immediately apparent that they like to roughhouse and, let's just say it, knock heads. They love to bash into each other, repeatedly. There is nothing like the sensation of a violent collision, as far as boys are concerned. If you need confirmation, ask their mothers. It has ever been thus.

Sometime in the 1820s, at Harvard and Yale, in the era before organized intercollegiate athletics, a tradition began. It was called "Bloody Monday." On the first Monday of the fall semester, sophomores would battle incoming freshmen in a version of a "football" contest. There was a ball in the form of a leather-bound animal bladder, and the objective was to bring it across a goal line. Otherwise, it was just more or less a brawl.

In their book, *College Sports: A History*, co-authors Eric Moven and John Thelin explain, "This lack of rules appeared to be exactly what the students wanted. Although scoring goals in those early nineteenth-century football games mattered, students also proved their mettle by kicking the shins and bloodying the noses of the members from the other class. The ability to take a beating and deliver one as well proved to be a sign of valor and strength."

By the mid-nineteenth century, these raucous events became notorious enough that they merited newspaper coverage. One New York reporter wrote, "The contending classes prepared for the game in the spirit of the [bull] ring. Boys and young men… knocked each other down, tore off the clothing, and, after the contest was over, eyes were bunged, faces blackened and bloody, shirts and coats torn to rags and shins broken." The administration and faculty of both Harvard and Yale regarded Bloody Monday as barbaric. Yale outlawed the tradition in 1857, and Harvard followed suit with a ban in 1860, just prior to a vastly more bloody event that commenced in 1861: the American Civil War.

Nevertheless, no edict from on high could dampen the growing enthusiasm at colleges throughout the Northeast for the game of football, in whatever form it took. On November 6, 1869, a group of young men from Princeton journeyed by rail to neighboring New Brunswick, New Jersey to face off with a team from Rutgers in what has traditionally been considered the first intercollegiate football game. The game more closely resembled soccer, with 25 men to a team and the objective of driving a round ball through a set of goalposts at opposite ends of a field that measured 120 yards long by 75 yards wide. Players could kick or hit the ball with their hands to advance it; they could catch the ball but not throw or run with it. There was no clock. The first team to score six goals would win. Rutgers prevailed, 6-4. There were approximately 100 spectators attending, the very first football fans. A grand tradition and spectacle that would, in a future time, come to capture America's attention like no other was born that day.

The situation became better organized by 1873, when Yale, Columbia, Princeton, and Rutgers held a convention in New York City and formed the Intercollegiate Football Association. Harvard refused an invitation to participate, instead focusing on the development of its own more rugby-like version of football. Harvard called it, "The Boston Game," which allowed for throwing and running with the ball, as well as tackling. Harvard found an opponent willing to play by the new rules in McGill University of Montreal. The two schools met in Cambridge twice in May 1874, Harvard winning the first match 3-0 and the second ending in a scoreless tie. To this day, Harvard football aficionados claim that those contests, not the Rutgers versus Princeton affair of five years earlier, represented the true birth of college football in America.

Though the rugby form of football gained in popularity, it was Yale and not Harvard that ultimately became the game's most influential force. Walter Camp, a New Haven resident who played football at Yale for six years from 1876 (he was eligible both as an undergrad and a medical school student) emerged as the "father of American football." Camp would go on to coach at Yale and, later, Stanford. His long-term impact on the game was profound.

Starting in 1878 and until his death in 1925, Camp served as the dominant member of the Intercollegiate Football Association's Rules Committee. Into the early 1900s, the sport remained terribly violent. In 1904, primarily because of the mass formation called the "flying wedge," 18 young men were tragically killed on the gridiron. In 1905, out of his desire to reduce the brutality and danger of football, President Theodore Roosevelt tasked Camp with continuing to revamp the rules with a special focus on making the game safer. Roosevelt advocated for football and his son Ted played at Harvard, but there was a growing movement to abolish the game entirely. Roosevelt intervened in hopes of saving the day. He needed Camp's help.

Over the course of his career on the Rules Committee, Camp worked hard to make the game better and safer. He pushed for such standards as 11 players per side and an offensive lineup consisting of seven linemen and four backs (a quarterback, a fullback, and two halfbacks). He also suggested that the ball be put into play by a center snap, rather than via a rugby-style scrum; the line of scrimmage thus came into being. He proposed the beginning of the "downs" system, which evolved into today's rule that a team has four plays to make 10 yards. With this innovation, white lines were painted onto the field at five-yard intervals, resulting in the term "gridiron." Camp pioneered the scoring system that ultimately put the focus on running or passing for touchdowns rather than kicking field goals. As a maker of rules, many of which we simply take for granted today, Walter Camp essentially invented modern football.

In its early years, the sport continued to gain in popularity with expansion to schools outside the Northeast, from coast to coast and north to south. In 1881, the University of Michigan became the first team from the Midwest to challenge the eastern powerhouses. Over five days that fall, Michigan succeeded in losing to Harvard, Yale and Princeton. One of Walter Camp's powerful Stanford teams lost a game to the upstart University of Chicago, which had only been founded in 1892. Chicago's coach, Amos Alonzo Stagg, was a Yale alum who had been an All-American football player on national championship teams. Stagg coached, taught and served as athletic director at Chicago for 40 years. In the process he built a football juggernaut and a system for developing and managing a big-time athletic program, one that would serve as a model for the future. Chicago came to be called "Stagg's University." Authors Moven and Thelin describe Stagg's considerable impact: "Often overlooked is that [Chicago] was a charter member of the Big Ten and for many years won the title of conference champion. Most important for the character of college sports nationwide, Amos Alonzo Stagg was the coach who created the structural protype of the intercollegiate athletics program."

Nevertheless, legendary empire builder though he was, Stagg did not win every time. One of the greatest moments in Carleton College sports history came in 1916 when, in true David against Goliath fashion, the lowly Knights pulled off an upset for the ages when they defeated the mighty Stagg and his invincible Maroon host from Chicago.

Members of the General Congregational Conference of Minnesota founded Northfield College in 1866. In 1870 the first president, James Strong, a Congregationalist minister, ventured to New England on a fundraising trip. After hitting up a wealthy Massachusetts manufacturer named William Carleton for money, Strong was seriously injured when a carriage in which he was riding was struck by a train. Perhaps out of pity, or because he was impressed by Strong's near-miraculous survival of his injuries, Carleton unconditionally donated the princely sum of $50,000 to the fledgling school. The Board of Trustees – no dummies, they - promptly renamed the place Carleton College. Carleton was a secular, co-educational institution from the beginning. The first two graduates, James Dow and Myra Brown, later married each other.

Records in the College Archive show that Carleton played its first football game in 1883. In that game touchdowns were worth two points, and the Knights prevailed over the University of Minnesota 4-2. From their inaugural campaign in 1883 and over the next 14 seasons, the Knights tallied a record of 22-14-1. In 1892, for the first time, Carleton faced future MIAC rivals Macalester and Hamline.

Max Exner was an outstanding football player who came onto Carleton's faculty as a physical education instructor in the 1890s. He became the advisor for Carleton's football "club" – football was not yet recognized as a varsity sport. Exner was instrumental in Carleton's transition from the rugby style to a more modern version of the game.

The fledgling sport continued to grow in popularity. In 1902, the school's first official varsity head football coach, Ernest Jones, took over and guided the program to a 7-4-1 record. In that same year, Carleton began play at Laird Field. Exactly a quarter century later, the grand old stadium building that still stands today made its debut.

A series of coaches followed until 1913, when the legendary C.J. Hunt became both athletic director and head football coach. Hunt is undoubtedly one of Carleton's greatest coaches. He led the Knights from 1913-1916 - during which time his teams went undefeated - then he left for the University of Washington. He was coaxed back to Carleton after World War I, in 1920, and coached the team for another decade. His career record was 75-22-4. His greatest moment came in 1916, when Carleton knocked off the Amos Alonzo Stagg coached and nationally ranked Maroons of the University of Chicago, 7-0. Carleton's team captain, "Stub" Allison, became a future C-Club Hall of Famer, as did Earl Keller, the man who scored the only touchdown on that memorable day.

Bob Sullivan himself very ably researched and wrote about the entire grand sweep of Carleton's football saga in his excellent book, *Knights of the Gridiron: A History of Carleton College Football, 1883-2005*, which he published in 2006 (we will cover his story of how that book came about in Chapter 17.) There is no need therefore for a detailed season-by-season, game-by-game recap of that history. But a few high points are worth mentioning.

First, and perhaps surprisingly given the topsy turvy, roller coaster ride that has defined Carleton football over the last six-plus decades, from 1883 until the late 1950s, Carleton produced winning teams virtually every year. Only one coach during that era had a losing record: in 1906, Dr. Newcomb Chaney coached the team to a 3-4 record. From the time of Ernest Jones beginning in 1902 until Mel Taube took over the program in 1959, there were 12 head coaches. Eleven of them had winning records; 10 of them had winning percentages exceeding .600; five won games at a .700-plus clip; from 1909-1912, Maurice Kent won 20, tied three and lost two for a winning percentage of .800. This was a highly successful program that demonstrated sustained excellence over more than 75 years. Carleton evolved into an elite academic institution while the football team thrived.

Second, the 1954 squad was arguably one of the best teams in Carleton history. Sully said in his book, "Two things became self-evident in 1954: first, that the team was destined for gold, and second, that while offense sells tickets, defense wins championships." The '54 Knights gave up only nine touchdowns and 59 total points all season. They held their opponents to 90.3 yards per game, best in the country at the small college level. Some of the many stars on this talented team included Captain Ted Smebakken, Bob Scott, Dick McAuliffe, and Dick Lindenkugel, all of whom were All-Midwest Conference honorees. The *St. Paul Pioneer Press* described Carleton as "the biggest surprise in Minnesota football this year." After returning home to Northfield from their final game of the year, a 20-6 win over Ripon that secured their perfect 8-0 season, the Knights were tired but exhilarated. Sully described the scene: "Years later, when asked what their greatest memory was from that season, almost to a man it was the spontaneous victory celebration on the Bald Spot and at the gym at midnight on the night they returned from Ripon. Faculty, students, townies, and parents were all there to welcome back the team. Curfews were suspended and the team was astonished at the outburst of support. 'Words fail us' was the thanks from the squad to everyone who took part in this night-time celebration."

Finally, perhaps the most interesting and memorable game in Carleton history took place in 1977. On September 17 of that year, 9,000 fans filled Laird Stadium to witness the first (and only) NCAA-sanctioned metric game in the annals of college football. The game was the brainchild of Carleton chemistry professor Jerry Mohrig. It received national coverage, including a mention in *Sports Illustrated* magazine. The field was realigned with metric markings and, in the game program, players' heights were given in centimeters and weights in kilograms.

The author played in that game; apparently, at the time, I was 175 centimeters tall and weighed 70 kilograms. Who knew? One additional draw was that the event pitted the Knights against our hated cross-town nemesis, the St. Olaf Oles. I caught three passes that afternoon as a split end, which was just about the only offense we mustered. I also jumped offside, again from the split end position, in a pro set standing wide left of the formation, where every one of the 9,000 spectators who was paying attention could clearly see me ("Was that the right guard that moved?"; "No, are you blind, it was that idiot receiver standing out in front of us; see him? He's right there!"). What ignominy… Oh well.

At halftime the score was 37-0 in favor of the Oles. They only scored once more but the final was still a demoralizing 43-0. Newly minted Carleton President Robert Edwards sat in the stands that frustrating day, dismayed by what he was witnessing, and reportedly said, "I've heard of de-emphasis [the phrase those who opposed football at Carleton used to describe what needed to happen with the program], but this is ridiculous." He was clearly embarrassed, and so were we. It sucked.

Nevertheless, it was an important game in Carleton sports history and, for those who participated directly, an unforgettable experience. The good news was that change would happen – President Edward's realization that Carleton College, paragon of excellence, did not excel in all fields of endeavor would soon translate into action.

On October 24, 1959, head coach Warren Beson, age 35, tragically suffered a fatal heart attack during the Monmouth game. With two games left in the season Mel Taube took over, and led the Knights for a decade, to 1969. He had an overall record of 33-47-3. There have always been elements within Carleton's faculty, administration and Board of Trustees who believe that football is barbaric, but it was during the mid-'60s to the mid-'70s that a number of powerful people were emboldened to speak out and advocate that the football program should be abolished altogether. Why would an elite institution such as Carleton, they argued, want to be involved in such a sport?

It was under these circumstances that Dale Quist, a local Northfield guy and football legend at Northfield High and the University of Minnesota, took over the team. Sully explained the difficulty of the scenario not just at Carleton, but in the world generally during that period: "Quist inherited what was probably the worst situation possible; the roster numbers were down, there was rampant anti-Vietnam War sentiment on campus, and the drug culture was in full swing. It took strong-backed people like Quist's first captains, Al Thiel and Jeff Bergquist, to keep football at Carleton afloat. The late '60s and early '70s were difficult times indeed for all of college football. The 1970 team went 1-8... 'We played for love of the game and the strong parental support we had was wonderful,'" said Thiel. Quist labored along but continued to preside over one dismal losing season after another.

With a career record of 20-56-1, by 1978, Dale Quist was done. President Edwards, and a lot of other people too, were tired of losing. Carleton College began a search for the successor who, also under extremely challenging circumstances, would take over leadership of the Knights in the fall of 1979.

CHAPTER 8

FOOTBALL GODS

Holtz & Walsh

"Lots of people can get into business, be successful, and make a lot of money. But when they die, their contribution ends. To have a significant, lasting impact, the key is to help other people be successful. Then your contribution lasts many a lifetime."

LOU HOLTZ

Bob Sullivan's primary mentors early in his football life were of course Tom Warner at Central Catholic High and John Gagliardi at St. John's. He learned a lot from both, and their influence was critical as Bob developed his own theories and methods as a coach. But his football journey was a long one, and he remained open throughout his career to new perspectives, innovative ways of thinking about the game, and the absolute requirement that he strive for continuous growth and learning as a teacher and coach.

Two coaches that he greatly admired were Lou Holtz and Bill Walsh. He became a disciple of both men. He listened to them speak, he read their books, and he followed their exploits. He met them both. In many respects, by the time he became an acolyte, Sully's coaching philosophy and processes were well developed. To some extent, studying Holtz and Walsh merely confirmed things he already knew. There was always a nuance, however, or a fascinating insight, or an inspirational quote that captured Sully's imagination and made him a lifelong fan of these two incredible leaders.

Sully recalled, "I went to a lot of football clinics in those days, at least two or three a year for sure. And I heard many, many coaches speak. Those two guys, in particular, captured my attention, my fancy. They were both smart, funny and thorough. They spoke to the same vibe or philosophy that I already had and made it flower, so to speak. They both had a huge impact on me, primarily in terms of my thinking about offense. Neither one of them was a football cliché, like so many other coaches are. I talked to both of them, by the way, just to introduce myself. They don't remember me, but I sure remember them."

At one clinic, Sully was scheduled to speak immediately after Walsh. When Walsh's allotted time was up, he said, "I'm not done." He spoke for another half hour. Sully was thinking that no one in their right mind would stay to listen to him when it was finally his turn - plus it was lunchtime. He was correct in his assumption. But no sour grapes; Sully chuckled: "I actually thought it was funny."

Sully's conclusion about Holtz and Walsh: "They just appealed to me, where I was and what I was doing."

Lou Holtz, Bill Walsh and Bob Sullivan all came from humble beginnings. Holtz was born on January 6, 1937, less than three months before Sully, in a small steel mill town in West Virginia called Follanbee. The family was poor, life was spartan in Follanbee, and young Lou learned the values of hard work and discipline. The family eventually moved to East Liverpool, Ohio, where Holtz became a football-loving boy when he attended his first college game in 1946. Like Sully, he was raised Catholic and fell in love with Notre Dame. In his autobiography, *Wins, Losses, and Lessons*, Holtz said, "Of course it was hard not to be a Notre Dame fan in those days. From 1946 through 1949 they played some pretty good football. Coach Frank Leahy was a revered figure in our home, one I would learn to respect even more after I got into coaching.

Leahy had seven undefeated seasons in fourteen years, a pretty stout record even by Notre Dame standards. As a kid, I settled down by the radio to hear most of those victories." Also like Sully, Holtz was an undersized but enthusiastic athlete: "I became a football player myself, an eighty-pound wonder boy who made up for his lack of size by being slow and weak." Unlike Sully, Holtz actually did go on to become the head coach at the University of Notre Dame.

Holtz never amounted to much as a player, but he had the makings of a coach from the get-go. In reflecting back on his junior and senior seasons in high school he said, "I never did anything outstanding, but I tried to be a good teammate. I played blocking back in the single wing, the old-style offense with no quarterback, two lead blockers, and half a dozen running plays to either side of the line... I did nothing spectacular in either of those seasons, but I did learn a lot by subconsciously studying my coaches. You can learn a lot by observing as well as performing. When I was in the huddle, I knew everybody else's assignment as well as the technique everyone needed to employ... The big difference was that I wanted to learn football." Holtz's head coach, Wade Watts, saw this budding interest and talent and encouraged Holtz's parents that Lou – an indifferent student - should go to college and get into coaching. They were surprised but agreed that college was the right path. Young Lou Holtz was on his way.

After an uneventful college football career as a linebacker at Kent State, Holtz considered becoming an Army officer but knew that his true passion was football. Commencing in 1960, he held a series of assistant coaching jobs over a nine-year span at Iowa, William & Mary, Connecticut, South Carolina and Ohio State. He got his first head coaching job in 1969, at William & Mary. He moved to North Carolina State in 1972. He went to the NFL in 1976, for a disastrous one-year stint as head coach of the New York Jets.

Recognizing that pro football was not for him, he returned to the college ranks and spent seven seasons at Arkansas. There was a brief two-year interlude at the University of Minnesota. During that time, when you could look up someone's number in a phone book and then call him at home on a land line, Sully rang up the Holtz residence. Mrs. Holtz answered. Sully introduced himself and told her that he was interested in joining her husband's staff as an assistant. Beth Holtz politely thanked him and hung up. He never received a return call.

Notre Dame came calling for Holtz in 1986. He went undefeated and won a national championship in 1988. He retired after the 1996 season, but was coaxed back to coach South Carolina, from 1999 to 2004. His career head coaching record was 249-132-7. Holtz was known as a turnaround artist, and for his robust sense of humor ("I don't ask people things. I tell them. See, I'm the coach.") He was a tough disciplinarian, but his players knew he had their best interests in mind; more than anything, he wanted them to go on and lead productive lives as good citizens. He is the only coach in history to lead four different teams to a top 15 ranking, and the only coach to take six different programs to a bowl game. He is in the College Football Hall of Fame. After his football career ended, he made a fine living as a keynote speaker (spouting mainly platitudes, interspersed with occasional words of wisdom) and worked off and on as a TV analyst. Lou Holtz is still alive and well as of this writing.

In terms of football philosophy, Holtz developed a reputation as an old school guy, for the primary reason that he liked to run the football when other teams were airing it out. His 1988 Notre Dame championship team was known for pounding the football down their opposition's throat. Like any good coach, however, he also demonstrated flexibility throughout his career and knew when it was time for a fresh scheme. For most of his coaching career he ran a twin veer offense, which allowed for some passing but primarily emphasized the running game as the quarterback reads the defense and distributes the ball accordingly (more on the attributes of the veer offense, which Sully also employed, in the next chapter).

When he arrived at South Carolina in 1999 Holtz told his offensive coordinator and son, Skip, that they needed to go back to the drawing board. An article from ESPN.com at that time described what happened: "Lou Holtz walked into a staff meeting, explained what he wanted in a new offense, and told the group, 'put it together.' The staff started from scratch, brainstorming ideas from their different backgrounds. It formed quite a thick notebook. 'He basically said, OK, this is broke. How do we fix it?' Skip said. 'And to tell him that time will handle it is not an answer. He doesn't want to hear that. He wants to know what he can do, how we can change things. You can't tell him it's going to heal itself.'" The result was a wide-open offense, featuring plenty of passing, which was highly productive.

Defensively, Holtz's primary go-to scheme over the years was Cover 3. This defense divides the field into three deep zones, with the cornerbacks covering the outside thirds and the free safety defending the deep middle zone. Four players (three linebackers and a strong safety) cover underneath the deep guys. Cover 3 is generally effective against both running and passing plays. In the book, *Defensive Football Strategies*, Coach Steve Bernstein says, "The primary objectives of the [Cover 3] defense are to stop the opponent's running game and to keep opponent's gains – whether by run or by pass – to a minimum (bend, but don't break)." Indeed, one drawback is that the defense can be vulnerable to an effective short passing game.

At South Carolina, again, Holtz had to adapt as he and his staff worked to turn the program around. He adopted a defense called the 3-3-5 Stack, which features three down linemen (Holtz inherited a tough and talented noseguard and chose to build around him), three linebackers, and five defensive backs. This defense is extremely effective in countering the kind of air-raid offenses that were common by the early 2000s. It caused confusion with variable blitz packages and tended to put lots of pressure on the quarterback. Along with the new, improved and wide-open offensive package, the Stack defense helped Holtz turn the South Carolina Gamecocks into winners. Among the many things that Bob Sullivan admired about Lou Holtz, his flexibility, adaptability and willingness to consider and adopt new concepts in the interest of winning, had great appeal and a significant impact.

Bill Walsh was born on November 30, 1931, in Fremont, California, during the darkest days of the Great Depression. Walsh's father, like Sully's, left school after the eighth grade to find work wherever he could. He suffered an extended period of unemployment during the Depression, finally securing work on an auto assembly line when Bill was young. Times were tight for the Walsh family, Bill's father was distant and cold and, his son said later in life, "a lout" who was hardly any kind of a father at all. In his biography, *The Genius: How Bill Walsh Reinvented Football and Created an NFL Dynasty*, author David Harris says, "Bill would nevertheless credit [his father] for instilling the 'work ethic' that would later be the staple of Walsh's football career."

Like Sully and Holtz, Walsh became a sports and especially football-obsessed kid. He played running back at Hayward High School in the San Francisco Bay area. His mother, who was an anchor and inspiration to him, wanted Bill to be the first member of the family to graduate from college. He enrolled at San Mateo Community College, a two-year school, across the bay, where he quarterbacked the football team. He then followed a girl to San Jose State (he didn't marry that girl but ended up meeting his future wife, Geri, after his first year), where he had a profoundly important educational experience.

Bill's new head football coach at San Jose, Bill Bronzan, was a true innovator and ahead of his time - like Sully's early mentor John Gagliardi. Harris explains, "[Bronzan's] teams pulled guards, blitzed safeties, ran the option, split the ends, and used three-receiver sets before anyone else on the West Coast... 'He had a great football mind [Walsh] remembered. He was a theorist and an excellent teacher who set a standard as to the detail of everything he coached and the organizational system he set up. He coached football like it was a science, a skilled sport instead of just head bashing.'... Bill himself would eventually credit Bronzan for his own decision to become a coach."

Bill was better known at San Jose for his boxing prowess than as a football player. He was talented enough as a fighter that he briefly considered becoming a professional, but he knew his first love was football. After graduation, he served for the next two years as a private in the Army at Fort Ord in Monterrey. He was married and a father by the time of his discharge, and boxing seemed a difficult and dangerous career. That left only one option: football.

Like Sully, Walsh began his career as a high school head coach, making a championship team out of the Huskies of Washington Union High School

in Fremont, California from 1957 to 1959. In 1960, he left to become a receivers coach at Cal Berkeley. The next stop was Stanford from 1963-1965
as a defensive backs coach. By this time, Walsh was deep into the process of
deciding what kind of coach he wanted to be. He attended as many clinics
as possible during the offseason, networking and learning his profession. He
was a devoted student of film study. Harris quotes him: "There was this religion of 'toughness' in coaching circles in those days, and all coaches were
trying to be like Marine drill sergeants and scare people into playing well. I
got caught up in that for a while but I concluded it didn't come close to working. It was a kind of mass delusion. All the coaches thought the players loved
them despite how badly they treated them, and all the players were doing was
putting up with the coach so they could play football. Instead of loving and
revering the coach, they couldn't stand him and were disgusted with him...
They wanted the fellowship, they wanted the association, they wanted the excitement, and only put up with the bullying because they had to. Most played
football in spite of the coach... I decided that if you taught people to play the
game better, that was real coaching – being a teacher rather than a 'thug.'"

Walsh's first taste of the NFL came as a running backs coach with the
Oakland Raiders, in 1966. The stop in Oakland was significant in that Walsh
was exposed to Al Davis's wide open, deep-vertical passing offense. Davis
had been a disciple of the great Sid Gilman, who was famous in the '60s as
coach of the San Diego Chargers for slinging the ball down the field. Gilman
had an excellent quarterback in John Hadl and one of the all-time greats at
receiver, Lance Alworth (known as "Bambi" because he had a baby face and
ran like a deer). The exposure to this unique offensive philosophy made a
deep impression on Walsh.

In 1967, Walsh served as head coach of the San Jose Apaches for their
one and only season in the Continental Football League – the Apaches dis-
solved in 1968. From there, he became an assistant to the legendary Paul
Brown of the Cincinnati Bengals, working under his tutelage from 1968-
1975. Many expected that when Brown vacated the head coaching position
to focus full time on his responsibilities in the front office of the Bengals that
Walsh would take his place, but it was not to be. Walsh spent one season as
the offensive coordinator for the Chargers, and then it was off to another head

coaching job in 1977, but in the collegiate ranks at Stanford. He spent only two seasons there. In 1979, Eddie DeBartolo Jr., the young and impetuous but exceedingly ambitious owner of the San Francisco 49ers, took a flyer on a 47-year-old football lifer who had never been a head coach at the NFL level, and hired Bill Walsh.

The rest, as they say, is history. From 1979-1988, Walsh turned the 49ers into one of the all-time football dynasties. He coached them to six division titles, three NFC championships, and three Super Bowl victories. He won 10 of his 14 post-season games, was the NFL coach of the year twice, in '81 and '84, and achieved an overall record with San Francisco of 102-63-1. He is a member of the Pro Football Hall of Fame. Walsh passed away at the age of 75 in 2007.

Bob Sullivan believes that Bill Walsh was the greatest football coach who ever lived. Many others do too.

An internet search to find out anything about Bill Walsh's defensive philosophy generally leads to either nothing or explanations about how opposing defenses strove to stop him offensively. Indeed, he was an offensive mastermind par excellence.

The system that Walsh designed became known over time as the West Coast offense. In the book, *Blood, Sweat and Chalk: The Ultimate Football Playbook: How the Great Coaches Built Today's Game*, author Tim Layden explains, "The West Coast offense... was the first passing strategy in football to effectively attack the field from sideline to sideline rather than from the line of scrimmage forward... the Walsh offense used running backs as receivers in more extensive ways than any attack before it and, perhaps most significant, validated the short pass as an effective offensive weapon when most previous systems [such as the deep-vertical, throw-the-bomb offenses designed by Sid Gilman and Al Davis, for example] had lived and died by the long ball."

Walsh developed his system while working as an assistant to Paul Brown, one of the great innovators in football history, in Cincinnati. Super Bowl-winning coach Brian Billick recalled that era: "At that point in time, the league was knee-deep in power running and taking deep shots down the field. Bill really introduced the concept of using high-efficiency intermediate passing routes as basically an extended running game." Timing was critical in the West Coast attack; there needed to be precise coordination between the quarterback and his receivers. Also, in this attack, the quarterback had as many as four receivers to throw to – the QB's accurate reading of progressions was imperative. When linebackers blitzed against him, Walsh sent running backs into the void left by the blitzers. The offense spread the field horizontally in ways that had never been tried before. Finally, as Billick observed, the short, quick hit passing game accomplished the same purpose as an effective running game. This was an incredibly difficult offense to stop.

In addition to his prowess as an offensive innovator, Walsh hugely impacted the game in other ways too. He was a detail-oriented fanatic who scheduled his training camp and regular season practice schedules down to the minute. He believed teaching skills is the foundation of coaching. He focused only on skills that his players needed to demonstrate in a game. He did not overtrain, nor did he believe in having his players beat each other up in practice. He treated them with respect. He insisted his players call him Bill. He was accessible but also tough; he kept his distance from his players. He demonstrated humor when he thought it was appropriate. He thought football should be fun.

Everything he did, from his practice regimen, to game planning, to the logistics of team travel involved discipline and meticulous attention to detail. Steve Young, who along with Joe Montana was one of two Hall of Fame quarterbacks that Walsh coached, summarized, "Bill is the one who put it all together. He executed all of it, from how we're going to practice, how we're going to travel, how we're going to watch film – all of it. It was 'We're not gonna do stupid stuff. We're gonna make it simple, useful.' So yes, there are a lot of pieces to it. He actually brought it all together."

The 49er's organization served as a model for the rest of the NFL, and for football coaches everywhere, such as Bob Sullivan, who studied Bill Walsh and his methods.

How, specifically, were Lou Holtz and Bill Walsh important to Sully? "Well, they were both amazing offensive thinkers. Walsh, especially, was a passing genius. He was a pass first kind of coach. Holtz, on the other hand, was a run first and pass second guy, with that whole option offense that he ran at the time. He believed in the importance of running the football and in that, I side with Holtz. I always thought that a balanced attack was best."

Sully continued, "Both of these coaches, and all good coaches for that matter, evolve from what they thought originally to what they thought five years later, or five years after that. Football coaches, the great ones anyway, all evolve. Over time, they are never what they were when they started. These guys reinforced the need for reinvention; you can never stay the same over time. For me, I evolved a new philosophy at least every five years. Everything about football, which I love of course, has to involve new ideas. Things like film analysis, how and when you go about it, to how you handle your assistants, to how you deal with the players personally. That was very important to me, especially at Carleton, where I got to coach really great kids, smart kids, and good people too."

CHAPTER 9

THE ULTIMATE CHESS MATCH

Philosophy & Schemes*

"With the veer offense, footwork, mesh points, and landmarks are precise and unchanging. Each of the movements of the quarterback, dive back, and running back are carefully choreographed and measured... Precision and timing are the benchmarks used to measure the success or failure of the system."

FROM COACHING THE VEER OFFENSE, BY GEORGE THOLE AND JERRY FOLEY

Oxford Languages defines philosophy as "the study of the theoretical basis of a particular branch of knowledge or experience," such as "the philosophy of science." *Merriam Webster* tells us that, "philosophy is the systematic study of ideas and issues, a reasoned pursuit of fundamental truths, a quest for a comprehensive understanding of the world," and/or "a study of principles of conduct."

---

* *This chapter is for serious football nerds. Readers who are not football obsessed, if they so choose, may proceed to the next chapter.*

A scheme, *Oxford Languages* says, is a "large-scale systematic plan or arrangement for attaining a particular object or putting a particular idea into effect," such as "a clever marketing scheme." *Merriam Webster* defines a scheme as "a plan or program of action, especially a crafty or secret one" and/or "a systematic or organized configuration; a design."

With respect to football, an internet search reveals a slew of definitions. Here is a good one: "A football coaching philosophy is the blueprint that outlines a coach's core beliefs, strategies, and objectives. It serves as the foundation upon which all coaching decisions are made. This philosophy encompasses the style of play, team culture, and the development of players both on and off the field."

The concept of a football scheme is quite simple: "A set of formations and plays that dictate how players position themselves and execute offensive or defensive plays. The goal is to gain yardage and score points." (Or, conversely, to stop the other team from gaining yardage and scoring points).

Years ago, my wife and I were watching a game on TV and she declared, "I just don't understand football." I answered with words to the effect, "It's really simple: football is a violent physical struggle for control of ground." And it is that, but it is also so much more. In its' nuances, details, and aesthetics, football is endlessly complex, fascinating and forever evolving. There is a reason why football is far and away the most popular sport in our country. It is indeed "America's Game." A football game represents the ultimate chess match between coaches.

This is why the best coaches are, in effect, PhDs, and their branch of knowledge is football. They are incredibly intelligent men who could have been highly successful in any career they chose. But they love football and are deep students of their profession. They spend their entire lives in an ongoing, never-ending quest to develop a coherent, compelling philosophy and dynamic, battle-winning schemes.

Bob Sullivan's concept of a football philosophy was to always remember that it is an ever-evolving sport, and that he needed to keep evolving with it. His idea was that if you were stagnant, you would be left behind. He envisioned a fundamental evolution that would happen, both offensively and defensively, at least every five years, if not more often. Much of his reaction to the evolution would depend on the athletes he had to coach. He believed in adapting his philosophy and schemes to the capabilities of his players, rather than the other way around. "It's about the players, not the plays."

In his book, *The Q Factor: The Elusive Search for the Next Great NFL Quarterback,* former Super Bowl-winning head coach Brian Billick summarized what happens, over time, to NFL head coaches who get fired because they refuse to adapt and evolve: "If... coaches lose their jobs when their old ways of coaching sputter, why don't they change, or try to change, before they get the pink slip? Some are stubborn. *I'm smart. I know what I'm doing. Look at my record.* Some are too old. *I've always done it this way. I'm not chasing some fad.* And some don't know how. *Huh?"*

Coach Sullivan possessed a clear understanding of the need to embrace new philosophies and schemes. He was also a great student of the history of the game. "Football has always changed over time depending on who is winning. It is very much a copycat sport. When you think of how the game has evolved offensively, for example, in the old days teams ran the single wing; then it was the double wing; there was the straight T and then the wing T; the I formation, the wishbone and the veer, then the whole complicated piece about running an option offense out of multiple formations. The forward pass became legal in the early 1900s, but it wasn't until the '60s that teams really started to throw the ball. Today the shotgun is a big deal, because of the emphasis on passing. That whole thing had to evolve too, and it took decades."

Sully explained, "You have to go with the times. I attended clinics, did my reading, and learned from other coaches [such as Warner, Gagliardi, Holtz and Walsh]." Regarding disciplined study, Sully still has in his possession two well-worn books from over forty years ago: *Attacking Modern Defenses with the Multiple-Formation Veer Offense,* by Steve Axman, and *The Explosive Veer Offense for Winning Football,* by Jim Wacker and Don Morton (who later became head coaches at the University of Minnesota and University of Wisconsin, respectively).

Sully had obviously read and reread these two books almost to tatters. They are full of copious notations, made in his almost illegible left-handed scrawl, and underlined/highlighted passages. The worn, yellowing pages contain countless football play diagrams, and the books almost resemble a volume of *Euclid's Elements of Geometry* that has been examined and analyzed, ad nauseum, by a most dedicated scholar. He was Professor Sullivan, a learned man in his field. The best football coaches truly have an intellectual bent; they love to study their profession.

Sully's target throughout his career was to run 50 percent of the time and to pass 50 percent. He believed in a balanced attack as the ultimate goal. But, as a practical matter, he had to do what worked. When he landed his first coaching job at Hill, Sully was obviously fresh from his St. John's and John Gagliardi-influenced experience. So, his approach was basic with an emphasis on a simple, straight-ahead veer running attack, although he used multiple formations and occasionally put a man in motion. His Hill teams ran the ball approximately 70 to 80 percent of the time. The defense was also a St. John's scheme called 52 read, with five down linemen and two hovering linebackers.

When he got to Cooper, he decided to open things up a bit in the passing game, because he had the athletes to do it. He passed 40 percent of the time, while other teams in the Lake Conference were averaging no more than 20-30 percent passing. This approach won Sully and the Cooper Hawks a share of the conference title in each of his final two seasons.

When he arrived at Carleton, he really let loose. "You remember Jeff, you were there [I do remember, vividly; we did some slingin' of that ol' pigskin]. We came out throwing. We were the most pass-oriented team in the Midwest Conference. We used multiple formations, we put men in motion. And we threw the football."

For the most part, Coach relied on the tried-and-true twin veer offense, at least part of the time, with variations depending on his personnel, for the duration of his career. He never went entirely away from it.

Recognition for the invention of the veer generally goes to former University of Houston coach Bill Yeoman. For what it is worth, the College Football Hall of Fame gives him credit. In a 2007 article from the *Minneapolis Star Tribune*, local sportswriter Chip Scoggins interviewed Yeoman. The coach explained that the creation of the veer was serendipitous; the Houston Cougars were preparing for Penn State in 1964, when they set up a new formation with their two running backs split, each one lined up in the backfield four yards deep, directly behind the guard in front of him. They ran a few plays and saw interesting potential in the blocking scheme.

The basic idea with the veer is that the quarterback reads defensive players and then, based on what they do, makes a quick decision to take advantage of mismatches or misalignments. It is called the veer because the frontside halfback "veers" slightly to the outside as the quarterback moves down the line of scrimmage and puts the ball in his belly. If the defensive tackle – who is unblocked and free to decide who to attack - moves for the quarterback, he hands it off. If the defender goes for the halfback, the QB keeps the ball. When he keeps the ball, he can either run it himself or he has a third option, again depending on the reaction of the defense, which is to pitch the ball to the trailing halfback, who has accelerated into open space and then sweeps around end. Not surprisingly, the veer is sometimes also called the triple option offense.

Blocking techniques for the veer can vary, but frequently feature isolation of specific defenders, double teams, and efforts to create and take advantage of predictable reactions from the defense. The veer allows linemen to avoid blocking one and sometimes two defenders, frequently the opposition's best defenders, and make them wrong in whatever they do. If the defender goes one way, the ball goes the other. Another advantage of the veer is that it can be run well with undersized linemen, which is frequently what Sully had at Carleton. In the veer, linemen don't need to block for long periods of time. It is a fast-hitting offense and smaller, quicker linemen can block effectively in this scheme.

While many coaches who favor the veer, such as Lou Holtz, are generally more run-oriented, the offense also lends itself nicely to the passing game. Obviously, play-action passes, where the QB does what he normally does, fooling the defense into thinking run, work well. The QB can also sprint out, which puts pressure on outside containment and gives him a good view of his receivers downfield. Dump passes and quick screens are also effective out of the veer.

Run well, the veer offense can overcome athletic deficiencies. Yeoman explained his original idea: "I wanted the quarterback to do a better job with his read than the tackle did with his defense. What precipitated this [offense] was, we didn't have the [talent] to go around blocking Ole Miss man on man. And Auburn and Penn State." What the Cougars did have though, was swift and skilled athletes at quarterback, running back and receiver.

Houston led the nation in total offense for three straight seasons from 1966. In 1968, they finished first in scoring offense. "Nobody could have more fun than we did," said Yeoman, a West Pointer who played for Earl Blaik at Army and a College Football Hall of Famer who won 160 games in 25 seasons. The veer offense soon became all the rage.

As it evolved over time, the veer concept came to be effective out of a variety of formations. The split-back version still predominated, but the veer was also run out of the wishbone (three backs in the backfield instead of two, in a wishbone shape). In the 1960s, '70s and '80s, among other programs, Texas, Alabama, and especially Barry Switzer's Oklahoma Sooners featured dominant wishbone attacks. The veer/triple option also works out of the I formation and even the shotgun.

Many high schools around America currently run the veer. At the collegiate level, the service academies of Army, Navy and Air Force still famously strive to defeat bigger, stronger opponents with the triple option offense. Teams such as Ohio State, Oregon and Arizona have run the triple option out of a spread formation with an inside zone blocking scheme that calls for the offensive line to move forward together to block an area of the field rather than go man-on-man against a specific defender. Well executed zone blocking creates momentum past the first level of the defense to the linebacker level. Again, with this scheme, the QB follows his blockers, reads the defense and either hands the ball off, keeps it, or pitches it.

Both Lou Holtz and Bob Sullivan loved the veer offense. At the end of his career, Holtz said, "If I was hired again somewhere, and they told me they wanted to win a national championship, I would immediately put in the option. The dumbest thing I ever did in my career was to get away from it. To this day, it is an offense that cannot be defended."

At the beginning of the offensive section of his playbook, season-after-season, Sully explained to his players the attributes of the twin veer:

"Why the Twin Veer?

Our offense causes the defense to cover the entire field and not just a portion of it.

The Twin Veer lends itself very well to the passing game.

You do not need the consistency that a normal offense requires because you will get quite a few big plays regardless of the caliber of the opposition.

We will be asking you to do things that you are physically and mentally capable of executing against everyone. Consequently, this will build up your confidence and respect for yourselves.

You will constantly continue to improve as a football team because with only six basic running plays in our attack, you will achieve better execution due to repetition. You will soon discover that you will be learning technique instead of assignment.

The Twin Veer is not a turnover offense, and you will not beat yourself. The two ways you beat yourself are with turnovers and missed assignments.

The defense will be required to be very disciplined against our offense."

A sound offensive philosophy, with the veer attack as the bedrock principle, coupled with schemes that evolved and varied depending on his roster, enabled Sully to win over many decades at both the high school and college level.

On defense, Coach primarily ran a 50 base, which he called 52 read. The 52 design has five players on the line of scrimmage and two marauding linebackers. You need a tough nose tackle and aggressive backers. The defense works well with smaller, quicker players who can hit gaps and move around rapidly to confuse the offense. The 50 also incorporates various blitz packages to make life further difficult for the opposing quarterback.

In the 52 read scheme, the five defensive linemen are often responsible for two of the gaps between offensive linemen, which is called "two gapping." They assess or "read" the situation and determine which of the two gaps the offense might attack and then they control or penetrate that gap. The linebackers also read their cues and fly to the football to make tackles.

For Sully, the 52 read then evolved to the 50 slide, where the defensive ends line up outside the offensive tackles and the defensive tackles "slide" to the inside of the offensive tackles for the purpose of controlling the B gap. These defenders are responsible for defending only one gap, which allows for more aggressive, straight-ahead defensive line play. When run effectively, the 52 slide can create pressure on the QB and also control the run.

In the secondary, at Carleton, Sully installed at least three or four different coverage schemes every year, which were complicated to learn but enabled the defense to disguise coverages. He did this because he could. "We had really smart kids, always, but my D-backs were an especially sharp group, who could do everything I asked, easily. I remember one time I had lunch with a DI coach from a major southern university. I was telling him about our different schemes in the defensive backfield and asked him about what he did. He said, 'Bob, my kids are so dang dumb that they can only run one kind of coverage, and even that is a challenge.'" Sully smiled at the recollection: "My guys were great."

Perhaps the best example of Sully "evolving" from one approach to another happened in 1991-92, with a story that began at the University of Washington. Under legendary Coach Don James, Washington went undefeated and won a national title in 1991. That team was known for stifling defense. Led by consensus All-American defensive lineman and disruptive beast Steve Emtman (who subsequently was chosen first in the next NFL draft), the Huskies defense allowed only 67 yards and less than 10 points per game.

They set multiple records, including fewest yards, first downs, touchdowns and touchdown passes allowed in school history. They trailed in a game only five times all season. The defense they ran was called the 46, or Bear defense.

After the '91 season, Sully and his newly hired defensive coordinator, Gerald Young, traveled to Seattle to study the Bear defense with Washington's coaching staff. In the fall of 1992, the Knights installed the new defense, which turned out to be an incredibly good decision.

The Bear was devised by Buddy Ryan in the late 1970s when he was defensive coordinator for the Chicago Bears. In *Blood, Sweat & Chalk*, Tim Layden explained what made the defense so successful: "It is effective largely because it 'covers' head-on the three interior offensive linemen with defenders, dramatically reducing the protection packages available to the offense because the center and both guards had to block one-on-one and could not move or help in another manner. Ryan also overloaded one side of the defense close behind the line, further confusing the offense as to which defenders might blitz. It is a high-risk, high-reward defense, with as many as eight defenders in the box and just a single high free safety."

The Bear was also known as the 46 defense, as designated by Ryan in honor of his talented strong safety Doug Plank, who wore uniform number 46. In the Bear, Plank – who was in effect acting as a linebacker - and a brother linebacker would position themselves at the line of scrimmage on the strong side of the offensive formation. The Bear was especially useful in short yardage situations because it clogged the middle with three down linemen; it also allowed linebackers to run free and make tackles (which is what linebackers get paid to do). The Bear was a damn tough defense to attack.

The 1985 Chicago Bears went 15-1 in the regular season, then destroyed every team in their path through the playoffs on their way to an overwhelming victory in Super Bowl XX. Their defense, which featured future Hall of Famers Richard Dent, Dan Hampton, Steve McMichael, and Mike Singletary, was arguably the best unit in the history of the NFL. They allowed only 12.4 points per game and sent nine of their players to the Pro Bowl. These were hard men, and their mad scientist coordinator had them running out of a scheme that complemented their talents perfectly.

When the Knights installed the Bear in '92, the results were dramatic, and a MIAC championship followed. Bob Sullivan demonstrated in his leadership approach the flexibility in thinking and openness to new ideas that characterized his career. Perhaps all of us can take a lesson from him in "evolution."

TWIN VEER TRIPLE OPTION OFFENSE

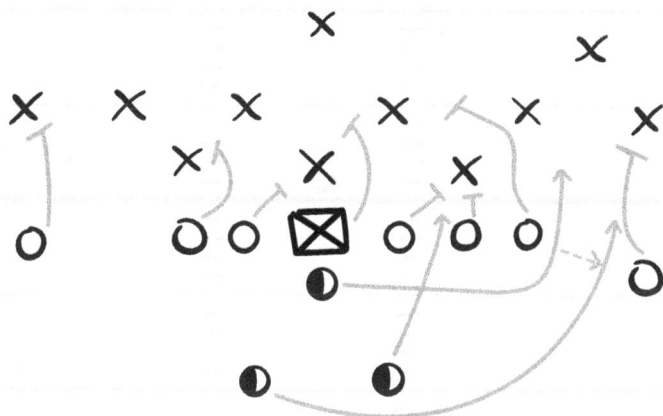

Sully relied on the twin veer offense, with variations depending on his personnel, for the duration of his career. The quarterback reads defensive players and then, based on what they do he either keeps, hands off, or pitches the ball.

LEFT SLANT DEEP ROUTE

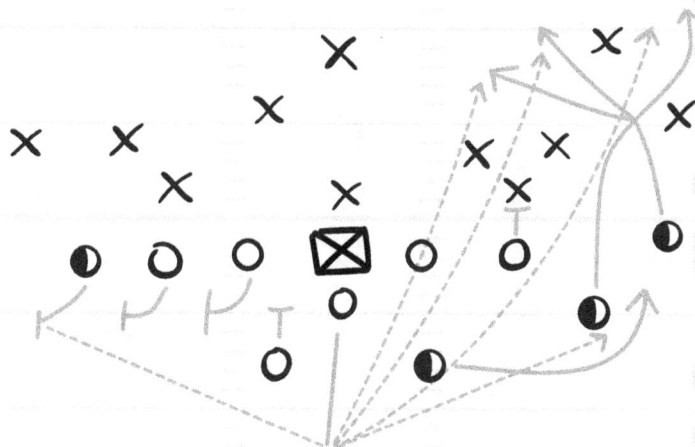

Sully's favorite passing play. The quarterback has deep and slant options, can hit the running back in the flat on a wheel route, or can dump the ball off to the weak side tight end.

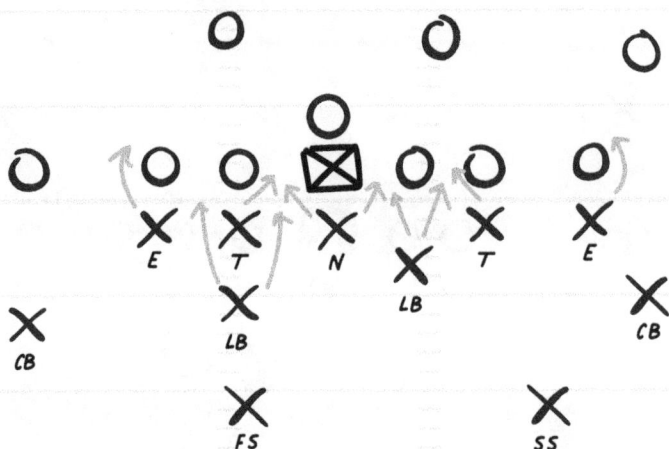

52 BASE DEFENSE

On defense, Sully primarily ran a 50 base, which he called 52 read. The 52 design has five players on the line of scrimmage and two marauding linebackers. You need a tough nose tackle and quick, aggressive backers.

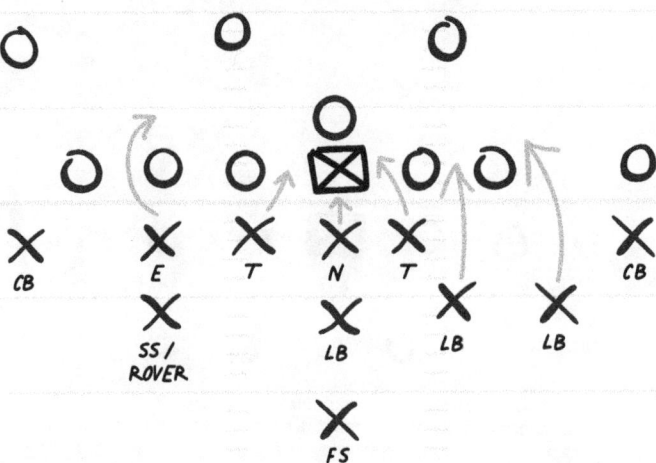

BEAR DEFENSE

In 1992, Sully installed the Bear Defense, and it helped the Knights win the MIAC championship. The Bear is a high-risk, high-reward scheme, with as many as eight defenders in the box and a lone free safety.

CHAPTER 10

1979

Beginnings

"The beginning is the most important part of the work."

PLATO

"Coaching is one thing and one thing only. It is creating an environment so the player has an opportunity to be successful. That is your job as a coach. When you teach him to do that, get out of his way."

CHIP KELLY

David Cade was a 1960 Carleton graduate and former football Knight who spent nine years teaching with Bob Sullivan in the English department at Cooper High School. Cade became aware of the head coaching vacancy at his alma mater in late 1978 and helped Sully position himself to interview for the job. In *Knights of the Gridiron*, Sully described what happened next: "The interview process connected with my hiring was very thorough. Virtually everyone was involved – from the current captains to the faculty, the administration, some students, and some alumni."

Sully was particularly impressed with Professor David Appleyard, who headed up the search committee. Sully said he had "never met a more fair-minded person" in his life. He also came away with great admiration for then President Robert Edwards: "He told me that my 'classroom' - the football field – was equally important as an academic field and that I should expect all the respect and attendance due in any other class. Edwards was a great fan and supported us in everything we did."

Within an hour of his hiring, Coach was on the phone recruiting Curt Wyffels. Curt had been a very capable quarterback at Park Center High, he impressed Sully when Cooper played against him, and he was an A student. Curt's first question: "Where is Carleton anyway?" At that point, if he didn't understand it before, Sully knew he had his work cut out for him. But he also well understood the ancient Chinese adage, "A journey of a thousand miles begins with a single step."

Unfortunately, only a few short months after Bob's hiring at Carleton in February of 1979, his beloved Shirley was diagnosed with Stage Four breast cancer. Priorities shifted dramatically from the challenges of a new job to the welfare of his family. Shirley underwent a mastectomy, then treatment and, happily, lived for another 30-plus years. But in that moment, the stress was unimaginable. Sully described the situation as both a difficult and exciting time for the family: "My oldest child Stacy had just graduated from Cooper High School and my oldest son, Tim, was slated to be the starting quarterback at Cooper, choosing to stay back and live with another family. We moved to Northfield without two of our children and my wife battling cancer. Shirley eventually underwent one year of chemotherapy treatment at Rochester Mayo Clinic and is a survivor."

Many people pitched in to help. Sully was forever grateful to one of his student managers, Tierza Wiese (who is today a successful medical doctor), who eased the family's burden by driving Shirley to and from the Mayo Clinic to receive her treatment. Together, through a very tough time, thanks in part to the kindness of others, the Sullivan family persevered.

On the football front, during the summer of '79, in addition to his recruiting efforts, Sully spent many hours in the College Library Archives researching the history of Carleton football. He studied game film from the previous season and concluded that there was a core group of talented athletes who would return to play for him in the fall. He met with each of those guys before they left campus for the summer and felt confident that the Knights would compete right away in the Midwest Conference.

Sully inherited assistant coaches Willard Tuomi (Tooms) and Jim Nelson (Nelly) from the previous regime. He hired Greg Hanks, who was a '77 Carleton grad and former team captain to be his defensive coordinator; Hanks proved to be an inspired choice and would be a great ally to Sully going forward. With the help of his assistants, and optimism in his heart, Coach got moving on building a winning football program.

Curt Wyfells quickly figured out that Carleton College is located in Northfield, MN, and decided to come play ball for Coach Sully. He became a terrifically versatile offensive weapon over his four-year career, eventually being named a winner of the Lippert Award, All-Conference and a team captain. Sully nabbed 14 recruits that year, including Wyfells, most of them from the Twin Cities, and several who had stellar careers. Karl Thomas and John Sieben were four-year starters at cornerback. Paul Vaaler and Bob Taylor starred at wide receiver. Tim Kruse made All-Conference at center as a freshman. These were ballers.

Sully also deeply appreciated the cadre of seniors he inherited: "I had a great group of 12 seniors who would prove to be wonderful leaders and eager students of the game. My first senior group included tri-captains Tim Franz [Franzie], Brian Davies [BD], and Mark Timmerman [Timmer]… The other seniors were Jeff Appelquist [App], Scott Wilhelmy [Scooter], Erik Moe [E-Moe], Zak Helmerich [Z-Dog], Phil Keithan [Monty], Tom Woodward [Woody], Mike Sullivan [Snake], Brad Schultz [Schwartz], and Tim Sommerfeld [Sommer]. [Please forgive the author for adding color commentary; here is absolute proof that this was an extremely tight-knit group; every guy had a nickname; we loved each other like brothers and still do to this day.] These 12, coupled with the 14 freshmen that I was able to recruit, would form the core of the 1979 team."

Years later, All-Conference strong safety Zak Helmerich talked about the commencement of the Sullivan era: "I remember Coach's first year and his first meeting with the seniors. We were a motley crew, but we were game and maybe most importantly, we were best of friends. There were some great young guns on that squad as well, and Coach went to work building his first team."

In the past, Carleton players who were science majors experienced scheduling conflicts between necessary lab time and afternoon football practices. These guys, of course, prioritized their lab work and were forced to miss practice. In an early demonstration of his ingenious flexibility, Sully told the boys to schedule their labs for Wednesday afternoon and then he arranged for the team to practice Wednesday nights under the lights at either Northfield or Faribault High School. Problem solved.

There were other changes as well, some significant, others subtle. Sully explained, "We also indoctrinated them with something I called the 'Psycholgy of Winning,' which they took to very well. We instituted the 'Team Prayer,' which everyone had to memorize and which we recited en masse just before hitting the game field on Saturdays... The players were more than willing to accept all of the concepts I had to offer and, well aware that I was teaching the cream of the crop intellectually, I didn't try to keep them on a tight leash... We ran a loose ship with only one rule: 'Tell the Truth.' Tell the truth to each other, tell the truth to your coaches and, above all, tell the truth to yourself. If you think about it, that rule really would cover all the mindless, nonsensical training rules that... many college athletes spend hours figuring out how to circumvent."

Practices were incredibly crisp affairs that commenced at 3:29 PM sharp. In his playbook, Sully outlined his practice philosophy: "We have a given number of concepts and schemes to cover in a given amount of time. Our practice time is two hours at the very most; we cannot afford to waste a single minute if we are to achieve our objectives each day. We will place a premium on organization and efficiency at all Knight practices this year. A snappy, well-planned 120-minute practice is certainly preferable to a 3 or 4 hour marathon." Players were not to miss practice. There was no sitting during practice. Players were to move quickly between drills. Poise was paramount. Enthusiasm and hard work were daily expectations. The boys could have fun, that was okay, but there was to be no horseplay.

It was eminently clear to every returning player: There was a new but, fortunately, beneficent sheriff in town. Things were going to be different from now on.

Despite the massive cultural shift and all the optimism, the 1979 season got off to a rough beginning. In the first game, the Knights lost 14-0 to Northwestern, a private evangelical school in St. Paul. Two key linemen, Captain Mark Timmerman and John Schlifske, both went down with season-ending injuries. Sophomore quarterback Billy Ford, a left-hander, showed flashes of his talent and potential in throwing for 229 yards, but the Knights nevertheless failed to score. Coach Sully expressed his frustration after the game: "It's really hard to get shut out running this offense. But we just did it."

The Knights also lost game two, their home opener at Laird, to Luther College, by a single point in a 17-16 nailbiter. There were signs of life and hope. But in the third game, the reality of what might become a lost season set in when the Knights were thoroughly thrashed by Augsburg, 34-6. It was a physical beat down in which four Carleton players had to be carried off the field. Sully remembered thinking at the time, "What have I gotten myself into here?" Fortunately, while the Knights sat at 0-3, these were all non-conference games. The boys could begin to redeem themselves starting with the next game, against conference foe Lake Forest.

At that time, the Midwest Conference was organized into two five-team divisions. In addition to Lake Forest, the pre-season favorite to win the division, Carleton's opponents would be Beloit, Grinnell, and the University of Chicago.

Steve Huffer, '81, was an All-Conference and honorable mention All-America offensive tackle. Years later, Huff had a very vivid recollection of the Lake Forest game, as the team sought to turn things around and was still in the process of evaluating the new coach: "Lake Forest was an away game and our conference opener. There had been some adjustment for the old timers to a new system and a new coach. The team never got comfortable in the first three games and played a little timidly. Mike Sullivan, '80, the other

'Sully,' [aka 'Snake'] brought his boom box to the game and fired up some Rolling Stones ('Satisfaction' if I recall) quite loudly in the locker room before the game while we were getting dressed. He had decided, quite correctly, that we needed something to get us into the right frame of mind. Coach came in and stopped and considered the situation as all eyes turned to him to see what his reaction was going to be. He said, 'Boys, I am a country music fan myself, but you can do whatever you think will help you get ready.' Nobody said it, but I know we all thought, 'This guy will be alright.' Well, we won that game and took it to them. It was the turning point of the season."

What Sully also characterized as "the biggest win of the season" literally came down to the last play. Carleton led 7-6 at halftime after a Bill Ford QB sneak and a Scott Wilhelmy conversion. The third quarter was scoreless. Carleton finally reached the end zone again on a 15-yard scamper by Eric Moe with 5:30 left for a 14-6 lead. The Foresters came back to score with 2:22 remaining and successfully converted the two-point try. Tie ball game. Lake Forest got the ball back once more, but gutsy freshman cornerback John Sieben made a clutch interception with about one minute to play. A run and then a passing play followed, to get the Knights in position for a 25-yard field goal to win. Tim Schoonmaker was a Carleton soccer star and sidewinder kicker in an era when a lot of guys like Scott Wilhelmy still kicked straight on, Lou Groza style. With just a few ticks left on the clock, Schoony lined that sucker up, took a deep breath, and cool as Wyatt Earp at the O.K. Corral, he drilled it through the uprights. Carleton 17, Foresters 14. Profound happiness and extreme elation erupted on the visiting sideline.

The next week, the Knights won comfortably at Homecoming, defeating Beloit 22-6. Bill Ford continued to perform well with 174 passing yards and two touchdowns. The Knight defense proved formidable, led by stalwarts such as linemen Bill Hoyt and Steve Sallstrom, noseguard Andy Engel, and safeties Zak Helmerich and Tim Franz, along with the two promising freshmen corners, Karl Thomas and John Sieben.

The next game was a bit too close for comfort, but the Knights again came away victorious. After building a 17-point lead, they had to scratch and claw to hang on for the 17-14 win over Grinnell. Brian Davies was stellar, with six receptions for 89 yards and a touchdown. He proved his versatility by adding three sacks from his position at defensive end. Eric Moe rushed for 96 yards, and Scott Wilhelmy's 30-yard field goal provided the winning margin. The Knights were now 3-3, with the opportunity to win the Blue Division of the Midwest Conference. All they needed to do was defeat the University of Chicago at home in two weeks. Thankfully, the Maroons of 1979 were not nearly as scary as they had been in the days of Amos Alonzo Stagg.

First, Carleton faced its crosstown nemesis, the St. Olaf Oles, in a surprisingly tight game at Laird Stadium. The Oles had consistently creamed the Knights, year after year in recent times; it became an embarrassment. But on this day, Carleton gave as good as it got. The Knights demonstrated their new-found grit by executing two determined goal-line stands in the first half. They were losing 10-0 when with 1:30 left in the half Davies caught a 55-yard bomb from Bill Ford. The two-point attempt succeeded, and the team went into the locker room at halftime down by only two. The Oles scored late in the third quarter and the Knights blocked the extra point attempt to put the game at 16-8. Carleton mounted a drive that stalled on the Ole eight-yard line. On the final play of the contest, with the ball at Carleton's two, the Oles called a timeout. Instead of doing the classy thing by taking a knee to end the game, in a gesture of truly rotten sportsmanship, they punched the ball over for one final TD. Final score: 22-8. The long-standing tradition of mutual hatred, contempt and general animosity between the two teams continued unabated.

In the final game of the regular season, the Knights took care of business by prevailing over Chicago 40-10. They put a spanking on the Maroons. Carleton had captured the Blue Division title with a 4-0 record and would play for the Midwest Conference title against the mighty Lawrence Vikings on an icy November 10th at Laird Stadium.

The game did not go well. After Carleton scored first early in the contest on a perfectly accurate, beautifully tight spiral from Bill Ford to Jeff Appelquist for a 29-yard TD, a deeply unfortunate thing happened: Lawrence got the ball back. The final score was 52-7. As Sully said, "Lawrence was clearly the better team, but the Knights had proven they were a force to be reckoned with." It had indeed been a fine season. Eric Moe led the conference in rushing with 612 yards. Billy Ford had thrown for 1,287 yards and eight touchdowns. Tim Franz nabbed five interceptions on defense. Ten Knights were named to the All-Midwest Conference team. Sully correctly concluded, "It had been a wonderful year."

In the summer of 2008, almost 30 years after the hard-fought inaugural campaign of the Sullivan era, a group of more than 30 players from the '79 team got together and assembled a scrapbook for Sully. The book contained pictures and news clippings, as well as a letter from each of the guys addressed to Sully, talking about what they remembered from that magical season. There were several themes that shone through in these missives, primary among them the hope that we all felt for the future of Carleton football; the need for discipline and preparation in the pursuit of excellence in all things; and the importance of positivity and thinking like a winner.

John Schlifske, '81, wrote to Sully: "I'll never forget our first team meeting before two-a-days started in August 1979. Two things immediately impressed me: (1) your optimism that we could build a winning program and (2) the organization your brought to everything. The fact that you had practices scripted so carefully, often down to the minute, showed me the commitment you had to doing things right." John went on to an outstanding business career and retired in 2024 as chairman and CEO of the Northwestern Mutual Life Insurance Company.

Captain Brian Davies, '80, told the Coach, "When we met, I knew that change was coming to the Knights. You brought incredible energy and a winning attitude to a program that was greatly in need of it. You also helped make football fun again, although some of that came with winning more games than we had before at any time in my four years." Brian also had a long and terrifically successful career in business, retiring as a top human resources executive with General Electric.

Finally, all the guys signed an introductory letter to Sully at the beginning of the book: "Through your enthusiastic and unswerving advocacy of a positive approach to life, you have influenced if not changed the course of innumerable lives among those you led on the field that year. Your leadership did much more than improve Carleton's fortunes on the field; your messages encouraged your athletes to hold themselves to much higher standards, to seek excellence through preparation in all endeavors (and to marry tall athletic girls who like football, and to maybe give country music a chance). These messages were really life lessons and not just instructions for winning on game day. Thank you, Coach Sully!"

CHAPTER 11

Opening Moves to Middle Game

"Teamwork is the ability to work together toward a common vision. The ability to direct individual accomplishments toward organizational objectives. It is the fuel that allows common people to attain uncommon results."

ANDREW CARNEGIE

Carleton's football record in the 10 seasons from 1980-1989 was a combined 57-40, for a .588 winning percentage. Continued strong performances in the Midwest Conference from '80 through '82 convinced the powers that be that the Knights could compete in the notably tougher Minnesota Intercollegiate Athletic Conference. Bob Sullivan enthusiastically advocated for the move. The first few seasons in the highly competitive MIAC were lean, but the Knights continued to build together toward a common vision. Their efforts would eventually pay off.

The 1980 season commenced auspiciously with the arrival of a whopping 25 freshmen recruits for August pre-season practice. For the first time in many years, the Knights enjoyed the luxury of a 60-plus-man roster. Exceeding the 60-player threshold would be the norm for the remainder of Sully's 22-year tenure. The only team after 1980 that fielded fewer than 60 bodies, ironically, was the 1992 MIAC championship squad.

The Knights collectively faced a serious non-football challenge when workers at Carleton in the maintenance, custodial and engineering departments went on strike. Sully explained the impact on the team: "For over four weeks we had to do our own laundry, scrub the showers, clean the locker room floors and line the football fields. My wife, Shirley, washed uniforms, towels and jockstraps at our home. We took cold showers for over two weeks before the boilers were turned back on." But as always, Coach chose to look on the positive side. "The entire experience proved to be another great opportunity for team building. The Knights became a stronger team as they worked together to deal with the sacrifices the situation demanded of them." Football teaches life.

While the Knights enjoyed a fine season, things may have turned out better had they not been racked by injuries. Among others, key contributors such as offensive tackle Bob Mackin and wide receiver Pete Gruman both suffered season-ending injuries. As a result, 11 freshmen saw the playing field at various points during the campaign. The Knights were young, but they were coalescing as a team.

The highlight of the season was a 28-18 win over Ripon at Laird Stadium, which was the Knights' ninth straight MWC regular season victory. After the game, the *St. Paul Pioneer Press* quoted Sully: "These are hungry kids, team-oriented, and easy to coach. I don't have the Mickey Mouse problems with them you have occasionally at the high school level." Sully reflected years later, "This quote could have been uttered in any one of my 22 years at the helm." Subsequent losses to Lake Forest and Lawrence put the 1980 Knights at 6-3, good enough for a runner-up finish in the MWC.

Throughout his Carleton career, Coach worked extremely hard to recruit the best student athletes he could find. Before the internet, social media and Zoom, he made phone calls, sent letters and traveled to meet with prospects face-to-face. He experienced special challenges in that he required athletes who would not only contribute on the gridiron but would also succeed in an elite academic environment. He needed to source special young men, and he focused most of his attention on Minnesota.

In *Knights of the Gridiron*, Sully commented, "While Carleton is a national school, the football team and the successes that it has enjoyed, will always be Minnesota bred… roughly two thirds of every Carleton roster was and is made up of Minnesota talent." Sully did some recruiting in other parts of the country, especially out west: "The out of state bonanzas have come largely from the West – Montana and California for example. Montana in particular was an absolute gold mine for me over all my 22 years."

In acknowledgement of the occasionally serendipitous, haphazard nature of recruiting, and the fact that a good deal of luck is involved, Sully joked, "Yes, recruiting is quite a science." Nevertheless, he did extremely well over two decades in drawing top talent to Northfield. "I knew I would be getting smart kids who were also great people – leaders, captains of their teams, easy to coach, quick to learn, and very motivated to succeed. They had a positive belief system which was a byproduct of their success in the classroom and on the field of play."

Troy Ethen, '88, described his recruitment experience, and the importance of Sully's personal touch: "One of the numerous things that made Coach Sullivan successful is that he truly cared about the well-being of his players. Though not likely developed as a means for these purposes, this genuineness helped in the recruitment and retention of players who viewed football as important, but not as the primary focus of their college experience. Personally, this made a difference. I had an elder brother drop his DII Scholarship upon becoming disillusioned with the focus on football over academics. It was clear in his recruitment that Coach Sullivan cared about what attending Carleton College would do for me and my professional career aspirations more so than what I could contribute to his football team. Both mattered. But my interests came first in his recruitment of me, through my four years and beyond."

Unbelievably, after the success of the '79 and '80 football seasons, certain elements on Carleton's campus began to question whether admissions standards had suddenly been lowered. As Sully said, "Concerns were being bandied about… as the result of recent winning by the athletic teams – football in particular, since it had been 15 years since the last winning football team at Carleton." How could a bunch of really smart guys also be good football players? Only dumb jocks were good football players. Everyone knows that.

Coach explained what happened next: "After much investigative reporting, the student newspaper discovered that, 'Smart athletes can win – and they do.' As Director of Admissions Jon Nicholson put it, 'When a football program turns around like ours has, people suspect that someone has been tampering with admissions standards. But the median SAT scores for this year's freshman class of football players are the same as entire class. Also, these players include two National Merit Scholars and four William Carleton Scholars.'" Sully concluded, "The 'investigation,' if that's what it was, was put to bed once and for all and students and faculty alike began to enjoy the success that comes from academics and athletics."

The 1981 club again featured an abundant and talented recruiting class. Twenty-nine freshman scholar athletes showed up in August. Among them were the future C-Club Hall of Famers, John Winter at wide receiver and Todd Kuss at linebacker. The team again achieved a winning record, finishing at a very respectable 7-3. The last team to get seven or more wins in a season was the undefeated MWC champion Knights from 1954, who were 8-0. Alas, despite their seven wins, the '81 Knights again finished as runners-up in the MWC.

Two games highlighted the season. In the opener at Laird Stadium, the Knights beat the Oles for only the second time in the past 18 cross-town contests. There were 5,000 spectators in the stands that day, and it was a monumental victory for the good guys. Spontaneous campus celebrations became the order of the day when the game ended. The final score of 20-12 brought the overall series to a very tight 30-29 in favor of the Oles.

In what Coach Sullivan regarded as one of the greatest games during his entire 22-year tenure, the Knights pulled off a stunning comeback in an epic battle that has gone down in Carleton gridiron lore as, "The Miracle at Ripon."

The Knights traveled to Ripon, Wisconsin to take on the Red Hawks on a muddy field with cold, wet, overcast conditions. The beleaguered boys in maize and blue were down 21-3 in the fourth quarter when things suddenly began to turn their way, as sometimes happens in both football and life, especially for those who think positively.

A series of clutch interceptions by Knight D-backs Paul Van Valkenburg, John Sieben and Karl Thomas, as well as stellar quarterback play by Billy Ford and key pass receptions by Paul Vaaler (two for touchdowns), Rick Kohlan and Mike Ostrum left the Knights with the ball on the Red Hawk 23-yard line. There were three ticks left on the clock. The intrepid warriors had one chance left. Cool as a cucumber, Bill Ford faded back and threw a strike to leaping freshman receiver John Winter for the tying touchdown. Jaws went agape. Kicker Dave Grein drilled the PAT. Final score: Knights 22, Red Hawks 21.

Bill Ford recapped after the game: "We knew we could win, and with only seconds left, everyone did everything right – the line and backs kept the rushers away, the receivers got to the end zone, Johnny Winter found a seam in the coverage, and I was fortunate enough to see him and fire it in there… The beauty of sport is that anyone who experiences a game like that in person never forgets it."

As a result of outcomes such as the Miracle at Ripon, Sully believed strongly that the Knights needed tougher competition. He stated years later, "If we had stayed in the MWC, and continued to get better as we did, we would have ended up winning the league title every year."

Out of his keen desire for a greater challenge, Sully sponsored a proposal to the Carleton Athletic Committee, chaired by David Appleyard, that Carleton enter the MIAC. There were several reasons why such a move made sense. The MWC was much more geographically spread out than the MIAC, and so travel costs and time spent away from campus would be reduced. Women's sports would benefit greatly since, up to that point, they essentially had no formal connection with any athletic conference. The MIAC move would give them good competition in every sport. The women's coaches were enthusiastically on board.

At the time, Appleyard commented, "There is no question that the MIAC schools are stronger athletically than the MWC teams.; the most visible sports like football and basketball will be affected the most." Sully didn't care. He was convinced that, "At a higher level of competition the players respond to whatever is there; they will just perform better." He knew his program was on an upward trajectory. He trusted his boys to battle hard, no matter who they lined up against. As of the fall of '83, Sully would get his wish, and the Knights would move to the MIAC.

With one more "lame duck" MWC season to go, however, a strong showing in 1982 would be important, and the Knights delivered just that. They continued their winning ways by going 6-2 overall, but with a 4-1 conference record, they were nevertheless frustrated to again be league runners-up.

Longtime head wrestling coach and assistant football coach Jim Nelson would retire after the season. Jim Christiansen, a local insurance executive and former Ole football player, had come on board as an assistant in 1980 and remained with the program for more than two decades. After the beloved Nelly left, Leon Lunder joined Sully's staff; he would serve for many years and later become Carleton's athletic director.

In a bizarre season opener against the Oles the Knights lost, 9-0. Carleton's first-string long snapper skipped the game that day because he needed to take his MCAT exams. Carleton is not Ohio State or Alabama; academics take priority. But his teammates truly missed the future doctor because, unfortunately, they lost the game after two bad snaps in punt formation. The first one, deep in Knight territory, resulted in an Ole safety, making the score 2-0. The second, also deep in Carleton's red zone, gave the Oles a TD that put the score at 9-0. In an additional strange and unhappy twist, Sully suffered a kidney stone attack after the game and became hospitalized for a week (this would not be the last time that Sully would be hospitalized after a loss to St. Olaf.) His summary at the time: "It was not a nice day."

One of the star freshmen who began the journey with Sully in 1979, All-Conference receiver and team captain Paul Vaaler, graduated in the summer of '83 with a prestigious Rhodes Scholarship in hand. Sully helped and encouraged him throughout the application process and was his biggest fan along the way. Paul went on to earn a master's degree from Oxford, a law degree from Harvard, and a PhD from the University of Minnesota. Today, Dr. Paul Vaaler is a highly respected professor at the U of M, teaching in both the law and business schools. He is a really smart dude.

So much for the theory that only dumb guys can play ball.

The year 1983 was significant in the annals of Carleton football. Of course, the Knights made their first foray into the mighty MIAC and, if the school archives are accurate, they had played their very first official football game in 1883; the sport had therefore survived and, during some eras but not others, thrived for an amazing 100 years at Carleton.

Sully and his young warriors immediately recognized that the going would be extremely difficult in the new conference. Among the 20 freshmen was future MIAC MVP and C-Club Hall of Fame member Dan Neinhuis, who starred at running back. At least a dozen of those freshmen would eventually start and contribute to Carleton's ascendance up the MIAC ladder, but it would take time and patience.

The boys ended the season at 2-8. Coach remembered: "The first MIAC contest was a brutal, physical football game... St. Thomas won 30-0 and was to go on to win the MIAC title with an undefeated mark posted by what was arguably their best team ever. In retrospect, I feel that if we had opened with anyone other than St. Thomas, we would have been fine. But we were in shock for two weeks..."

Also on the schedule for that season and, forever going forward, were the Johnnies of St. John's. The game held particular interest that year, for two reasons. As a result of Sully's tutelage under John Gagliardi during his undergrad years, there was a "student faces off against mentor" theme. In addition, Sully's son, Tim, played quarterback for St. John's. Sully recalled, "All of the newspaper headlines going into the game centered on these two themes. My wife, Shirley, was quoted in news stories saying, 'I've known Bob a lot longer than I've known Tim. For Tim, it's only a game; for Bob, it's a career. I am rooting for Carleton – loudly.'" Despite Shirley's best efforts at cheering the

Knights on, St. John's won the game 24-8. To his everlasting frustration, Sully would never defeat the Johnnies during his time at Carleton.

In 1984 the Knights continued to make what Sully called "baby steps" forward in their near-term objective of an upper-tier finish in the MIAC. They doubled their previous season win total with an overall record of 4-7. Guy Kalland joined the staff in '84 and became an excellent offensive line coach for Sully. Twenty-two freshmen joined the team that fall, including future C-Club Hall of Fame defensive end Troy Ethen.

The season started with a bang in a 45-0 blowout of Concordia-St. Paul. The Knights then defeated Augsburg 29-3 at Laird Stadium for the first of 11 straight victories over the Auggies. Sophomore wideout John Winter set a Carleton single-game record with an impressive 190 yards receiving. Among others, the Knights lost to their nemesis St. John's, St. Thomas, and a very good Hamline team that would win the league title that year. The Knights knew there were at least a few MIAC opponents that they could handle easily, they continued to think like winners, and they were gaining confidence.

As always, Sully was especially proud of guys like '84 quarterback Tom Shanley, who was one of only eight football players nationally who received a fellowship from the National Football Foundation and Hall of Fame for graduate study. Tom eventually attended medical school at the University of Chicago. Sully said, "As quarterback, Tom was truly the coach on the field. He had a tremendous grasp of the game and was a natural leader... but it was his intelligence and leadership that made him an outstanding athlete." Sully truly felt joy and happily called it out when his Knights excelled on the field, in the classroom, and in the game of life, which a hell of a lot of them did over the years.

Their inspiring motto the next season was "The Knights Will Arrive in '85." And they did, finally finishing in the upper tier of the MIAC with a 5-5 overall record. They won four conference games, which was good for a tie for third place.

Again, Coach recruited a bumper crop of 25 talented freshmen, what he called the "top recruiting class in Carleton football history at the time." Among many fine players, All-American and future C-Club Hall of Famer Tim Nielson would begin his career at running back but eventually lead the way as Sully's all-time best quarterback. Two of Sully's greatest ever offensive linemen, honorable mention All-America Guy Finne and Tommy Olsen, would become key contributors. On defense, Mike Stam, Dave Hoppe and John Heyneman were all extremely talented players.

The Knights clobbered the Comets of Concordia-St. Paul, 58-0, in the season opener. Dan Neinhuis scored three touchdowns, one rushing, one receiving, and one on a punt return. The defense gave up only 31 rushing yards. The Knights had made a statement, and they would be competitive in every game for the remainder of the season.

In a sound 31-13 thrashing of Augsburg, the Knights' D intercepted six passes, including two by Dave Adams, who would become Carleton's all-time career leader in interceptions. Again, run defense was stifling, giving up only 32 yards. The next week, the Knights were only down 10-7 against St. John's at the half. The game remained tight until late in the fourth quarter, when the Johnnies surged to win 23-10. This was discouraging but still represented genuine progress.

The Knights saved their best performance of the year for the Oles, a contest that has gone down in lore as "The Medallion Game." Sully explained his motivational technique: "At our final team meeting in November of 1984, after the seniors had left the room... I asked the remaining players to take a vow. I had purchased 55 medallions with 'October 19, 1985,' the date of the next St. Olaf game, engraved on the back. The team all agreed to take a vow to wear the medallion until that day. By taking the vow, the team swore to dedicate their off-season training and do everything possible to defeat the Oles the following season... The deal was struck, and the players and coaches alike were filled with a determination to see their goal was met." The final score on that historic day: Carleton 35, St. Olaf 7. The '85 freshmen would never lose to the Oles, and the Knights would win 10 of the next 11 Goat Trophy games.

Coach reflected on what happened the next season: "1986 would prove to be a watershed year for Carleton football, now in its fourth year in the MIAC. Knights' football would be a force to be reckoned with well into the 1990s as a result of the steady growth spurt between 1983 and 1986." A key freshman addition in '86 was Scott Bunnell, who hailed from Palo Alto, California, and was the Bay Area Athlete of the Year as a defensive tackle in football and a weight man in track. Scott could have gone DI, but for a variety of reasons chose Carleton instead. It was a recruiting coup for Sully, as Bunnell went on to become an All-American and C-Club Hall of Famer. A transfer from Augustana College in South Dakota, linebacker John Haberman became one of Sully's all-time best defenders. On top of the substantial talent already on the roster, these boys were ready to take things to a new level.

The Knights finished the season 7-3, their first winning record in the MIAC. The unquestioned highlight was a stunning 39-11 victory over mighty St. Thomas, a game characterized by MIAC pundits as "The upset of the decade." Some Carleton football historians asserted that it was the most important and shocking win since the Knights defeated Amos Alonzo Stagg and his Chicago Maroons in 1916.

Going into the game, the Tommies were ranked number one in their region of the NCAA, and number five nationally; they were seemingly without weaknesses and a true powerhouse. Knowing that a coach's primary responsibility on game day is to give his team the best opportunity to win, Sully made one of the most difficult and agonizing decisions of his career: he moved Tim Nielson into the starting quarterback role over established first-stringer Todd Nickodym. Todd had been an excellent QB and was a key team leader and captain; it was a hard call to make. Coach explained his reasoning: "Tim Nielson... was a player who needed the ball in his hands as often as possible since he could make a lot of good things happen and he almost never made a mistake. As a sophomore, he simply had to be in the lineup and touching the ball on every play."

With Nielson at the helm, in his very first start at QB, the Knights commanded the day. Nielson ran for 116 yards and two scores and threw for 140 yards and two more touchdowns. Tom Ferry rushed for 160 yards and a score. The Carleton defense was tough all afternoon, stifling the vaunted number-one-ranked Tommy offensive attack. Dave Adams intercepted two passes, and Billy Peterson recorded seven sacks.

The Knights just put a good ol'-fashioned ass-whippin' on 'em. Among other headlines, the *Minneapolis Tribune* trumpeted: "Nielson's start a success as Carleton upsets St. Thomas." The *St. Paul Pioneer Press* reported, "Carleton piles up 558 yards to rip St. Thomas." Sully's conclusion: "The win gave Carleton immediate credibility in the MIAC and set off a chain reaction which, among other things, shocked St. Thomas into losing their last two games as well, allowing Concordia, a team that Carleton should have beaten [the Cobbers defeated the Knights 21-14 at Laird in a hard-fought homecoming game], to win the MIAC crown."

In May of '86, *The Carleton Observer* published a piece called, "Carleton's Entrance Into the MIAC: A Third Year Review." The article stated, "Carleton athletes [since the move to the MIAC] now encounter a level of play that far exceeds anything they have seen in the past... By participating in a league that is intensely competitive, athletes have to dedicate more time to their sport... The implications of the switch have led some to ask if the college is now overemphasizing athletics at the expense of its academic reputation." The article examined the various reasons that Carleton had made the move, such as reduced travel time and expenses and the positive impact on women's sports.

The piece concluded, "So far, the switch to the MIAC has made the college stronger. As the coaches and administrators recognize, the determining factor... is the feelings of the athletes. What is good for Carleton athletes is good for the Carleton athletic program. So far, athletes like to move to the MIAC... As long as athletes think they can compete in the conference... then Carleton should stay in the MIAC and applaud itself for strengthening the college."

Ironically, prior to the St. Thomas game several months later, Coach Sullivan experienced considerable misgivings about the move to the MIAC. Despite the *Carleton Observer's* upbeat assessment of the change, Sully felt differently: "I was seriously thinking of going to the president and telling him that we had made a serious mistake by going into the MIAC, for if we had remained in the Midwest Conference, we most certainly would be winning a title with this team. I decided to wait until after the St. Thomas game... I almost felt like we were leading the lambs to the slaughter... but magic in the form of Tim Nielson would prove to be the difference maker."

While Sully had mixed feelings, he continued to believe long after his Carleton career was over that it was arguably a mistake to go to the MIAC. But after the perfect St. Thomas gem, he would not be expressing his opinion to the president just yet.

The 1987 team ended the campaign at 6-4, good for fourth place in the MIAC. This was the third straight season with a first-division finish in the league. Twenty-seven freshmen became Knights, including two who were destined to become Carleton greats: John Nielson, Tim's younger brother, and Tim Thull, a stellar D-back. Both guys were phenomenal all-around athletes and would end up in the C-Club Hall of Fame.

The season included highlight wins over Macalester and Hamline, as well as a third straight victory over the Oles, 37-18 at St. Olaf. Back-to-back losses to the Johnnies and the Tommies brought pain and frustration. Tim Neilson returned as quarterback and continued to play extremely well, ending the season as team MVP. As Tim's fortunes went, so went Carleton's offensive attack.

The Knights also fielded a star-studded defense, featuring such stalwarts as Troy Ethen, Dave Hoppe and Scott Bunell on the defensive line; John Haberman and John Heyneman at linebacker; and Tim Thull and Dave Adams in the secondary. One additional defender stood out: Mike Stam, known by his teammates as "Stammer," was a complete stud who continued to develop rapidly as his career went on. In '87 he absolutely dominated at defensive tackle, with 12.5 tackles for loss and 6.5 sacks, to bring his career total to 17. He was big, strong, fast, and getting better every day. Out of his dynamic performance in the fall of '87, he generated considerable interest from NFL scouts.

But in the off-season of 1987-88, tragedy befell Mike Stam. His devastated teammates would be forced, with profoundly sad and heavy hearts, to power their way through the next season without him.

CHAPTER 12

Our World Has Stopped

"By dying young, a man stays young forever in people's memory. If he burns brightly before he dies, his light shines for all time."

ALEKSANDR SOLZHENITSYN

I never met Mike Stam, but I would have loved to have played ball with him, had him as a teammate. By every account, he was truly one of the good guys.

There is a photo from the 1987 season of four Carleton football players in full pads, no helmets, taken on a bright, sunny day on the field at Laird Stadium. Mike Stam is the centerpiece of the image. Draped and apparently climbing all over him, like little boys on a jungle gym, are three of his teammates, Ben Edwards, David Lund and Tim Nielson. Ben sits suspended on Mike's right hip, David sits up high, legs straddling Mike's broad shoulders, and Tim sits on his left hip. None of these guys are as big as Mike, of course, but they are still college football players in full combat regalia. There is some considerable weight there. Mike holds them all up above the ground with ease, like a circus strongman. His legs resemble mighty tree trunks. He is not even breaking a sweat, shows no sign of strain. What he is doing is effortless for him. All four players are not just grinning; they are laughing out loud. You can almost hear their boisterous shouts. They love each other. They are teammates and brothers, and they will be forever and ever. They are experiencing great good fun and the marvelous gift of being young, strong and invincible. It is a wonderful picture of four vibrant men in the joyous and exuberant prime of their youth. They could not possibly be more alive.

Dave Hoppe (Hop) knew Mike Stam well. They came to campus together in the late summer of '85 and played on the same defensive line for three seasons. Dave explained, "We hit it off right away because we were both from small Minnesota towns – I was from Watertown-Mayer and Mike grew up in Faribault. He was a really good guy; I define a good guy as anyone who laughs at my jokes, and Mike definitely laughed at my jokes. He was really kind of a quiet, reserved guy, though. He would show up to campus parties but would be off to the side sipping his beer. He never made himself the center of attention."

Mike always intended to come to Carleton. The Knights would occasionally practice on the Faribault High School field on Wednesday nights during the season. In Mike's senior year at Faribault, he came to watch them all the time. He couldn't wait to become part of the team.

Mike was all about improving as a football player, which he did dramatically over his three seasons. He spent countless hours lifting weights. Hop said, "I remember that he worked at a small fitness center in Northfield, to earn a few extra dollars, and he would get up at some ungodly hour to go to work. Usually there was no one there that early, no customers, so Mike took advantage of the weightlifting equipment and got in his reps."

Mike Stam ultimately became a stud of a football player. "He got close to 270," recalled Hop, "which was an enormous DIII defensive tackle in those days. He could really move too; he was very fast for a guy of that size." Indeed, Stammer stood 6'3" and weighed in at 263 pounds. He ran a blistering (for a huge dude) 4.7 second 40-yard dash. In *Knights of the Gridiron*, Coach Sullivan marveled, "A late developer, Mike, while being a very good high school player, just kept getting better, bigger, and faster after arriving at Carleton. He was the most dominant defensive lineman in the MIAC in '87, when he was an All-Conference selection... Mike was indeed a pro prospect… we had two phone calls from lawyers wanting to become his agent."

Mike, of course, like all of us, was an imperfect human too. He was not above mayhem and mischief and the kind of extreme rough play and extra-curricular shenanigans that occasionally go on in a heated football contest.

In what would be the final game of Mike's career, against Bethel at the Metrodome on November 7, 1987, the Knights crushed the Royals, 45-0. Bethel, a private Christian university in St. Paul, was not all that good in foot-ball during that era. Consequently, to have any hope, they needed to throw the ball. This allowed Carleton's defensive front four to just pin their ears back and go for the quarterback. Troy Ethen recalled, "You know how these days, you can't just put your full body weight on the QB when you take him down? At that time, there was no such rule. Stammer fell heavily with his entire bulk on their passer. On the way back to the defensive side, he said to me, 'Troy, I think I might have ***ing killed the guy.' One of the Bethel players started yamming at Mike for what he perceived to be gratuitous and unnecessary violence. Stam shouted back, 'Hey! That's not very Christian!'"

Hop remembered the '87 game against Gustavus: "We were on the bot-tom of a big pileup, Mike and me, and the Gustie running back we had just brought to the ground, and a few other guys. You know how it's always the second guy in any altercation that the ref sees, and that guy is the one who gets the penalty? Well, this Gustie back is down on the ground screaming at the top of his lungs, 'They're twisting my leg! They're twisting my leg!' He gets up from the pile, furious, and he shoves Stammer. Mike looks at the ref, wide-eyed and innocent. The ref only saw the shove, so the yellow flag flew. Fifteen yards against Gustavus. Back 'em up, fellas. The kid's still going ballistic, shouting at the ref, 'They were twisting my leg at the bottom of the pile!' Stam and I get back on defense and I say, 'Listen to that guy. What a whiner. What the hell is he bitching about?' Stam leaned into me, smiled, and fessed up: 'I was twisting his leg at the bottom of the pile.'"

Mike Stam received his first-team All-MIAC plaque at halftime of a Carleton basketball game on Wednesday evening, January 20, 1988. He traveled to

Faribault the next day to be with his family to celebrate his 21st birthday on Friday the 22nd.

When he got home, he tinkered with his snowmobile and then took it out for a test run. While riding his machine, he was hit from behind by a train and killed, probably instantly. The exact circumstances of the accident were hard to pin down as there were apparently no witnesses on the ground. Did he become distracted or disoriented? Did he not hear the train coming? Did he try to outrun the train? No one knows. The only certainty was that the great Mike Stam was dead, one day shy of his 21st birthday.

The team was stunned. Years later, a group of his teammates came together on a call and remembered with sorrow how unbelievable the news was. When Troy Ethen heard a teammate say, "Mike is dead," Troy's first reaction was simply, "It can't possibly be true. Someone has made a mistake. Stam was utterly invincible. We gathered, all confused, at the Stadium. Then Coach Guy Kalland came out of his office. The look on his face told us it was true. Mike was gone." Dave Hoppe, John Heyneman, John Haberman, and Jamie Jurkovich lamented the shock of it. They all concurred: "We were all indestructible in those days, but if any of us was especially indestructible, it was Stammer."

Sully sadly recalled what happened next: "The funeral was on Saturday, January 23rd, at Sacred Heart Catholic Church in Faribault. The pallbearers were his teammates and roommates: Ben Edwards, David Lund, Pete Sickle, John Heyneman, Tim Nielson, and Todd Stevenson. The entire team and coaching staff was in attendance and it was, without a doubt, the toughest situation that the program and I ever had to endure."

Sully delivered the eulogy at a memorial service for Mike at the Carleton College Chapel on January 26:

"Our world has stopped. Everything in our lives has come to a standstill as we mourn and ponder the death of Mike Stam. Mike Stam, whose very presence suggested invincibility.

Mike was, above all else, a wonderful human being, a simply great young man... a shining jewel of a person.

Mike Stam was an outstanding and dedicated college football player...

He was, very probably, the best defensive lineman in Carleton history. Mike was totally dedicated to his goals and his dreams and was doing everything possible to fulfill those dreams at the time of his death...

Mike loved Carleton and he loved being here. Mike was a friend to all who knew him and was liked by all who knew him. Mike led a full and happy life in his twenty plus years and the only answer as to why he was killed is that God wanted him more... he was only loaned to us, and we are better for having known him. What we need to do is celebrate Mike's short life. Mike's life was a celebration of life, and he would want us to remember him in a joyful, positive tradition. He went out at the top of his game – Godspeed Michael."

Sully finished by reading a poem called *To An Athlete Dying Young*, by A.E. Housman, to which he added his own poetic quatrain at the end:

"But oh how strong you ran the race
With the wind forever in your face,
And those you left behind will know
Because of you their strength will grow."

Mike's family engraved this verse upon his gravestone.

The team grieved, heartbroken, but knew that they had no choice except to carry on. Never give up in the face of adversity, as Sully had taught them. They dedicated the '88 season – in which they achieved another successful 7-3 record - to Mike's memory, honored to be wearing his #74 on their jersey sleeves. They created a sign and placed it above the inside entrance to the field at Laird. It remains in place to this day, and Carleton football players ever since have touched it to gain strength as they march out to do battle each gameday Saturday. The sign reads: "Through these doors march the Knights – Champions of Carleton Football – In Memory of Mike Stam, 1967-1988."

There was discussion about retiring Mike's jersey, but the family thought a better idea would be to keep the jersey number, and therefore Mike's memory, alive. During the 1990 season, freshman defensive lineman Tom Jacobs of Nebraska became the first Knight to proudly wear number 74. The tradition continues to the present day. Michael Carey, an All-Conference defensive lineman, traded his previous number 66 for number 74 in the 2024 season, in honor of Mike.

A Mike Stam memorial began to bring in decent sums of money. Sully consulted with the Stam family, Mike's parents Chuck and Dianne, and his sister, Missy, concerning what to do with the fund. Mike always felt that linemen get short shrift, and don't receive the recognition they deserve (he was right about that.) In that spirit, MIAC leadership agreed to establish the Mike Stam Award, to be presented annually, starting after the '88 season, to the outstanding offensive or defensive lineman in the conference. Mike's likeness is engraved upon the coveted plaque, and there was great joy at Carleton when Mike's linemate, Scott Bunnell, another talented and ferocious defensive tackle, won the award in 1989.

Sully loved his 1992 MIAC championship team. He readily acknowledged their greatness. But he was never sure that his young warriors of '92 were his best team. In fact, he believed there was an argument to be made that the 1988 team, even without the mighty force that was Mike Stam manning the defensive front, was his best team.

Nineteen freshmen came on board in '88, including future C-Club Hall of fame honorees Jim Bradford and Jeff Scherer. Those two dynamic guys at wide receiver formed the best tandem Sully ever coached. Also joining the squad was center Geoff Morse, a future All-America. Tom Nielson, father of Tim and John, joined Sully's staff as an assistant, excited for the opportunity to coach his sons. He proved highly valuable to Sully over the next several years. Bubba Sullivan joined the staff as an intern. His football education continued.

Carleton dropped three games on the season, losing to Hamline, Concordia-Moorhead and, of course, the Johnnies. Unfortunately, the loss to St. John's pretty much ensured the Knights would not win a share of the conference title.

But there were a bunch of highlights. The boys defeated Lawrence – to whom they had lost three straight - in the season opener, 35-0. At Homecoming, they won the annual contest for the Goat Trophy, 25-7. It was the fourth consecutive victory over their detested cross-town rivals, which meant the '88 seniors never lost to the Oles. In *Knights of the Gridiron*, Sully recalled: "The win over Gustavus, 34-21, was probably our best game of the season. Nielson had a career day, again. I asked our statistician how many total yards we had and he kept saying '502,' and I said, 'That's a nice total,' and he said, 'No, I mean Nielson had 502 yards." Tim set a school and MIAC record that day with his 181 rushing and 321 passing yards. The Knights ended the season in the Metrodome with a smashing 31-3 victory over Macalester, which put Carleton's record at the Metrodome at 4-0.

Tim Nielson set numerous career and season offensive records and was named both MIAC and team MVP. He, along with teammates Guy Finne, John Haberman, and Scott Bunnell were first-team All-MIAC honorees. Nielson was named to several All-American teams and Finne made honorable mention All-America.

All in all, the brave and intrepid men who proudly wore the maize and blue in the fall of 1988 enjoyed great success in their commitment to honoring the memory of their beloved fallen teammate, Mike Stam.

When I ponder the death of someone like Mike Stam, an excellent human being who left this world, and all of those who knew and loved him, far too soon, I feel a range of emotions: sadness, certainly; perhaps some survivor's guilt; a sense of the fragility and injustice and unfairness and randomness of the universe; uncertainty, helplessness, and even fear in facing adversity and the whims of fate.

But I also feel a profound appreciation for the gift and the miracle that is life on this Earth. I feel that appreciation much more deeply as I get older than I did when I was a young man, in the halcyon days when I too was invincible.

I have a simple little prayer of gratitude that I repeat to myself every single day, and have for many years, usually when I step outside into glorious nature first thing in the morning to take my daily walk:

I am happy to be alive today
It's a great day to be alive
Every day is a precious gift
Tomorrow is not promised.
Amen

CHAPTER 13

1992

Champions

"Talent wins games, but teamwork and intelligence win championships."

MICHAEL JORDAN

The twenty-five freshmen who showed up for camp in the late summer of 1989 would enjoy spectacular success and close out their careers as champions. Among many others who achieved stardom for Coach Sullivan along the way were Ted Kluender at quarterback; placekicker Pat Bell; All-American Watie White at defensive end; and two All-America honorees and future C-Club Hall of Fame members, running back/tight end Scott Hanks and free safety Art Gilliland. Sully said, "These men would enjoy wonderful careers at Carleton and formed the core of the '92 team."

The '89 team ended up at 7-3, good for a third-place MIAC finish. One of the highlight games of the season came in the opener, when the Knights clobbered Lawrence, 35-14. Quarterback John Nielson (Sully's second-best all-time QB, behind only his brother Tim) set a school record with five TD passes. Stellar receiver Jim Bradford also set a Carleton record when he hauled in four of those passes for touchdowns. Nielson's performance earned him DIII Player of the Week honors.

The Knights stumbled against the Oles, losing 27-22 and giving up the Goat Trophy for the first time in four years. Carleton came back and regained their winning form against Hamline at Laird. The boys were down, 22-10, late in the game. John Nielson sparked the comeback with two TDs passing and another one rushing in the fourth quarter. Final score: Knights 31, Hamline 22.

The Knights lost to Concordia-Moorhead in a classic Homecoming matchup. Five thousand fans watched a back-and-forth battle that ended with the Cobbers on top, 34-26. The Knights were once again crushed by the Johnnies, 56-14, but they won the season's final two contests for the fourth straight time to finish in the MIAC's upper division for the fifth campaign in a row. For the season, both Nielson and Bradford set multiple passing and receiving records. Their pitch and catch routine never grew old. Overall, Carleton's record, as always in recent years, was respectable. But they were not yet championship contenders.

The 1990 season was somewhat bizarre. The good news was that freshman Adam Henry, who would become Sully's best all-time running back, joined the team. The bad news was that, very uncharacteristically, the boys dropped the first five games of the year, but by only 29 total points. They were all nail-biters.

Offensive statistics were off the charts. The team averaged 33 points per game, but this was not enough to prevent them from losing to UW-Platteville, St. John's (in a frustrating squeaker, 36-35, that was lost when two controversial calls went against the Knights in the final three minutes), Concordia, Hamline, and St. Thomas. They sat at 0-5. An opposing coach labeled Carleton the "best winless team in America."

But in a dramatic turnaround, the Knights ran the table for the remainder of the season to finish at 5-5, for their sixth straight upper-division finish. The boys finally began to get their act together against Augsburg in a convincing 49-7 victory. In a scoring extravaganza at Laird, they easily defeated Gustavus, 49-32. Nielson broke his own record for touchdown passes in a game with six. He set a single game mark with 456 passing yards while also breaking the career TD pass record with 32. Not to be outdone, Bradford also set records with five TD receptions in a game, 285 receiving yards in a game, and 19 career TD catches.

A win over the Oles at Laird, 37-20, brought the Goat back and tied the historic series at 34-34-1. The season's grand finale could not have been better. Facing a very tough 7-2 Bethel squad at the Metrodome, the Knights staged an epic 80-yard drive with less than two minutes remaining. With no timeouts, they ran 11 plays to score and win the game, 31-30. Sully proudly recalled, "It was one of the best drives in the history of Carleton football and would go down with the '81 "Miracle at Ripon." This team, despite their deceptive .500 record, had scored 331 points on the season, to become the first Carleton team ever to score more than 300.

Sully summarized the end of an era in '90: "Six successive seasons with a Nielson at quarterback had come to an end after one of the most successful and record-setting runs in Carleton football history. Both Tim and John had rewritten the record books and led Carleton football to the upper echelon of MIAC football... Carleton had a 62 percent winning record, with 37-23 over that time and a 32-22 MIAC mark... It had been a nice run and one which put Carleton on the map in one of the top (if not the top) conferences in DIII football."

Carleton's fortunes went from bizarre in 1990 to disappointing in 1991, as the team suffered its' first losing season since 1984, finishing at 3-6, good for seventh place in the MIAC. There were still several high points. Sophomore quarterbacks Ted Kluender (who had taken a year off to get his academic house in order – he still had three years of eligibility remaining) and Ryan Beckers competed for the starting job. They both saw action and played well during the season, with Kluender eventually becoming the starter. Teddy would go on to set numerous passing records during his storied career. Beckers was an outstanding athlete who subsequently transitioned to receiver and made significant contributions catching rather than throwing the ball. Twenty-five freshmen joined the team, including Brad McDowell, who would develop into one of Sully's all-time best at tight end.

The most important game of the year was a stunning upset of defending MIAC champion Concordia-Moorhead, on their field, 30-20. Adam Henry flashed a glimpse of his future greatness with 209 rushing yards that included a 54-yard scamper to seal the deal in the fourth quarter. That sideline dash capped a drive that had started at the Carleton one-yard line. An interception by free safety Art Gilliland stopped the final Cobber's offensive series. The Knights pummeled Augsburg, 59-7, at Laird for Homecoming. The boys set a record for total offense in a game that day, with an incredible 632 yards.

The Knights' third and final victory of the campaign was another wipe-out, 40-0 over Macalester on Parent's Day at Laird. The highlight of that day was a conference-record setting 98-yard TD pass from Kluender to speedster Jeff Scherer. To the great disappointment of the team, the St. Olaf game had to be canceled due to the historic weather event known throughout Minnesota as "The Great Halloween Snowstorm of '91." More than 28 inches of snow accumulated during this mega storm, bringing everything in the state, including scheduled football games, to a screeching halt.

Jim Bradford ended his extraordinary four-year run in 1991 second on the DIII all-time list with 3,710 career receiving yards. He had broken every Carleton receiving record and several MIAC records and was named a first-team All-America. His buddy and running mate Jeff Scherer made honorable mention All-American. It was fitting that Willard Tuomi, Tooms, retired at season's end after an astounding 37 years coaching receivers at Carleton, ending his career along with the best tandem of pass catchers he had ever had the honor to coach.

The 1992 season began with a completely fresh look on defense for the Knights. New defensive coordinator Gerald Young had traveled with Sully to Seattle to spend several days with the staff at the University of Washington. The Huskies were fresh off a national title-winning run. The mission for the Carleton coaches: study the fearsome defense that had stifled nearly every team Washington faced. Sully remembered, "We then came home and put in the new defense, which was called 'G Scheme' with some Chicago Bear '46' thrown in as the changeup."

More than three decades later, quarterback Ted Kluender marveled: "You think we were good on offense that year, and we were. But it was our defense that won the championship for us. I ran against that Bear D every single day in practice, and it took me probably a month before I had it figured out. It was that challenging trying to read what the hell they were going to do. Can you imagine another MIAC team that only has four or five days to study film and game plan against us? Everybody was baffled. Our D was just excellent all year long."

On offense, Kluender had come into his own. Balancing a lethal passing attack with the running of Adam Henry, who had led the team in rushing the previous two seasons, the Knights were formidable. Teddy estimated that the team probably ran 60-65 percent of the time and passed 35-40 percent. Scott Hanks was key to the passing game after switching from running back to tight end. He ended up leading the nation in receptions for a tight end. Sully justifiably patted himself on the back later: "What a genius move that turned out to be." He was right (as baseball pitcher Dizzy Dean once remarked' "It ain't braggin' if you can do it.")

Although the '92 team was smaller in numbers, with less than 60, it was top heavy with upper classmen, including 17 seniors. Only Chris French at fullback enjoyed significant playing time among the freshmen. Experience played a huge role and tipped the scales in favor of the Knights all season long.

Another important factor in the team's success was that they played the full season, until the playoffs, pretty much injury free, which is a rare feat in college football. Sully said, "The stars must have been aligned because we were able to start the exact same lineup in all 10 regular season games..."

The season started with a bang. The Knights destroyed non-conference foe Northwestern-St. Paul, 49-3, to notch the College's 400th football victory, only six fewer than St. Thomas at that time. It was an auspicious start. The MIAC season began at Laird with a 36-0 drubbing of Hamline. In a harbinger of things to come, the new D allowed only 137 total yards, with minus one rushing yard. The Knights then traveled to Bethel and, despite being down early in the game, came back to defeat the Royals, 24-14.

The much-anticipated Homecoming contest with St. Thomas drew 6,000 excited fans to Laird Stadium. As always, the Tommies were tough and talented, but the Knights prevailed, 25-20. Kluender threw for 223 yards. Nine of his passes went to Hanks for 150 yards. Adam Henry rushed for 137 yards. Once again, the Knights' offensive attack was balanced and effective all day. The following week, Carleton went to 5-0 with an easy 32-6 victory over Macalester. After that game, national ranking services named the Knights as the fourth best team in the Midwest region.

The Goat game with those friggin' Oles drew 4,000 fans to the Scandinavian side of the tracks. The Knights won, 21-9. After the game, Scott Hanks spoke for the whole team when he said, "We prepared better for this game than any other. In the back of our minds there were those eight seniors from last year who didn't get to play due to the Halloween snowstorm... Last year's season was tough and when we didn't get to play the Oles it really upset the emotions. It feels great to beat them." Carleton was now seven out of the last eight against St. Olaf. The win also put Sully's career total at 75, which tied him with the great C.J. Hunt.

Sully looked to become Carleton's all-time winningest football coach the next week at Laird versus Concordia. The Cobbers were 5-1 and anxious to get the victory and back into the MIAC title chase. They almost succeeded. The Knights were down 14-zip in the first quarter but came back with three second quarter touchdowns. The Cobbers scored again and led 21-20 at the half. A third quarter pass from Kluender to Henry put the Knights ahead for good, but there would still be some heart-stopping thrills. With the score 26-24, Carleton, the ball rested at the Knights' nine-yard line. On the game's final play, Concordia had one last chance to win with a chip-shot field goal. But Aston Coleman burst through the Cobber defense to block the kick. For his heroics – he also had a key interception earlier in the contest – Aston was named MIAC Defensive Player of the Week. Years later, when asked to identify the highlights of the '92 season, Ted Kluender said, "Well, winning the championship of course. But a close second was Aston blocking that kick against the Cobbers. We went ballistic. It was just a great moment."

With a win the next week, 38-28 over Augsburg, the Knights went to 8-0, the first time such a record had been achieved since the 1954 MWC champs finished their undefeated season, almost four decades earlier. The '92 guys were truly chasing history.

The next week proved disastrous. Cold, snowy, muddy conditions at Laird forced the annual showdown against the Johnnies – who were 6-1 - to be moved to the Metrodome. Sully remembered regretfully, "Once again, the Pupil-Mentor theme between myself and John Gagliardi drew a lot of attention in the press as well as the dream matchup... 15,000 fans were at the

Dome... In what proved to be a disaster, humiliating and an aberration, St. John's took advantage of penalties and turnovers to demolish the Knights, 70-7, and provoke numerous emotions from both camps."

But all was not lost, and Sully and his young warriors refused to give up. Fate handed them a gift the next week. On November 14th at the Metrodome, St. John's at 7-1 and Concordia at 6-2 were playing to potentially tie for the MIAC title. Miraculously, the game itself ended up in an 18-18 tie. There were no sudden-death overtimes in those days. A tie was a tie and it was still, as one old football coach once said, "like kissing your sister." The tie, as Sully recounted, opened up "the glorious possibility of winning the crown outright with a win over Gustavus [who the Knights would play in the final game of that evening at the Dome]."

In the game, Carleton scored all its points in the first half to lead 21-14 at halftime. The vaunted Knight defense would have to hold on to ensure victory. Again, there would be thrills. Adam Henry uncharacteristically fumbled a Kluender pitch to turn the ball over with 2:10 left on the clock. Sure enough, the Gusties scored with 32 seconds remaining, making it 21-20. In a gutsy Gustie move, they decided to go for the win from the one-and-one-half yard line. In a defensive play for the ages, Neil Volker picked the right gap to attack, shot through, and hit the Gustie QB before he even took a step. Knights win, 21-20.

Pandemonium erupted. Sully got carried off the field. The boys went en masse straight to a downtown Minneapolis establishment. One of the proud fathers put $200 on the bar and asked the barkeep how much it would buy. The friendly server said, "Don't worry, I'll just keep 'em comin'." The Knights more than deserved their celebration.

The party was short-lived, however, as the team now needed to prepare for Carleton's first foray into the NCAA DIII playoffs. They would travel to Pella, Iowa, and their opponent would be the formidable Dutch from Central Iowa. For the first time all season, Carleton suffered a string of injuries to key contributors. Wide receiver Aaron Cox was hurt in the Gustavus game; in Pella, fellow receiver Ryan Beckers injured his ankle on a muddy field during pre-game warmups; and star free safety Art Gilliland got hurt in the game and missed most of the second half.

With a lineup that Sully adjusted on the fly, and extremely difficult field conditions, the Knights lost, 20-8. The Knights were a speed team. Sully lamented the lack of solid footing for his fleet backs and receivers: "Tripping and slipping were the order of the day as beauty and speed were not in the game plan... To this day I firmly believe that if the game had been played on a dry field we would have won." Disappointment aside, it had still been a glorious season.

The Carleton Knights had won more games than in any single season in school history. It was the first championship of any kind since the '79 divisional-winning campaign, and the first outright conference crown since 1954. Sully summed up the significance of the magnificent, magical 1992 season: "All kinds of accolades, publicity and good things happened for the team after the championship. Congratulatory letters, phone calls and honors came our way as the unlikely championship stirred many peoples' emotions... With Carleton's academic rigor and reputation overshadowing everything in sight, to win the football championship was doubly gratifying."

CHAPTER 14

And Baseball Too

"Oh and, by the way, ahem, maybe I forgot to mention, you will be the head baseball coach too, just so you know."

CARLETON ATHLETIC DIRECTOR JACK THURNBLAD TO A SURPRISED COACH SULLIVAN, THE INSTANT THE INK WAS DRY ON THE FOOTBALL CONTRACT THEY HAD JUST SIGNED IN 1979

"Can't anybody here play this game?"

CASEY STENGEL, MANAGER OF THE 1962 NEW YORK METS, WHO LOST A RECORD 120 GAMES IN THEIR INAUGURAL SEASON

B ob Sullivan was a good baseball man, and a good baseball coach. The very first sport he ever played as a boy was baseball. He was a good player. His baseball acumen was good; he understands the game. He coached baseball at Hill High School, and they had some good teams. He has closely followed the trials and tribulations of the Minnesota Twins, who have been sometimes good but rarely great, ever since the team formerly known as the Washington Senators relocated to the Twin Cities in 1961. He likes baseball. He has always been interested in baseball. Yes, Sully was a good baseball man.

But he was a great football man, and a great football coach. And therein lies the difference.

There is no detailed chronicle of the history of Carleton baseball. No *Knights of the Diamond* as a counterpart to Sully's own excellent *Knights of the Gridiron*, which does such a fine job of telling the long, grand story of Carleton football. Therefore, specific information regarding Knight baseball teams, players, and stats over the years is extremely hard to come by.

There is an additional problem: neither Sully nor most of the guys who played for him remember much of this stuff either. We have a bit of a vacuum there.

Suffice to say that Sully coached baseball for at least some of the years he was at Carleton; in other years, someone else coached the team when, for example, Sully took a spring sabbatical or took time off to attend football clinics. Most notable among that group was Tom Nielson, who as Carleton's head baseball coach had the wonderful opportunity to coach his two sons, Tim and John (who were just as good at baseball as they were in football). Tom coached the Knights to a MIAC title in 1991, which was the height of achievement for the baseball team during that era. Most of Sully's teams, both in the MWC and the MIAC, were second-division finishers.

What people do remember well is a whole slew of good Sully baseball stories, several of the best of which follow. Some of these stories will be told in the first person, others will paraphrase what several guys said on the same subject. Key contributors to this chapter were Mike (Snake) Sullivan and Scott (Scooter) Wilhelmy, '80; Bob (Brado) Bradovich, '82; and Brent (Brently) Siegel and Jon (Darbs) Darby, '83.

Here we go.

During one baseball practice, Sully decided there would be an intrasquad competition, to hone the team's skills in a game situation. Sully announced the rosters for Team A and Team 2 (???). He shared two key pieces of information: A) Sung Yeon Yim would bat 12th for both teams (last we checked there were only nine batters allowed per side in any given baseball game); and 2) "Moss" would not play (problem here was that there was no player named Moss on the roster, as we shall soon find out). Jon Darby summarized what the team was thinking: "That made no sense on many levels, but we played the game anyway."

There was a player named John Young on the team. John was a good guy, everyone liked him. For some reason, Sully kept calling him "Moss" for at least the first two or three weeks of the season and no one corrected him. During practice one time the team was gathered around Sully as he tested them on the signs he would be giving as the third base coach. He would give the steal sign and ask, "Siegel?" Brent would answer, "Steal," correctly. Then the bunt sign. "Godfrey?" Sully would ask and Tim would answer correctly. Then Sully gave another sign. "Moss?" No answer. "Moss?" Again, no answer. "Moss?" as Sully looked at John Young and asked, "That is your name, isn't it?" John said "No, it isn't." This after weeks of John participating in baseball practice. Hmmm.

During one game, Pete Rizik was a runner at second base and stole third, except he did not have the steal sign. As he slid hard into third, he broke the ankle of the opposing team's third baseman. Sully loved the collision and despite missing the sign, Riz became Carleton's starting third baseman. Aggressiveness was good in football, and in baseball too.

Jon Darby was the runner on third base and saw Sully give the suicide bunt sign. So did the batter. All good until the batter missed the bunt attempt and Darby was hung out to dry running full speed toward home plate. In those days players were allowed to crash into catchers to knock the ball loose and that is exactly what Darby tried to do as he lowered his shoulder and plowed into the catcher. Unfortunately, the catcher managed to hold on to the ball as the collision flipped Darby head over heels. Sully ran toward home plate yelling, "What the hell are you doing?" Darby told him that he (Sully) had given the suicide squeeze sign. Sully replied, "Oh... w'hell, you showed me something with that collision." Aggressiveness was good in football, and in baseball too.

Early in the spring, at the beginning of each season, Sully and the team would pile into a bunch of vans and/or cars and drive south, to do a swing through several warm weather states and play a few baseball games along the way (what could possibly go wrong with that scenario?) This was always good prep for the upcoming campaign.

During one spring road trip, Mike Sullivan rode with a group of teammates and their car broke down en route. Snake hitchhiked from Merrillville, Indiana, and made it to Americus, Georgia, in time to pitch the season opener for the Knights.

Snake remembers, "For the trip back to Northfield, the three of us who had been stranded ended up squeezing into the cars available, and as luck would have it, I got to ride with the Sullivans for the 19-hour trip back. We left early at 5 or 6 am. Coach and wife Shirley sat in the front and took turns driving. I sat in the back with Bubba and Molly. My reputation had preceded me a bit, and a couple of 'looks' from Mrs. Sullivan told me to watch my salty language and jokes around the kids. She was very nice and cordial but there was a streak of Mama Bear in her that I recognized and didn't dare to cross."

Bubba Sullivan was 13 at the time and Molly was 10. Bubba recalled the road trip well: "Mike was really funny, trying to make us laugh in the backseat. Telling stories. I think my mom gave him a look when he tried to teach us the lyrics to a bawdy song, which he obviously thought was fun, but she did not believe was 'age appropriate.' Things quieted down after that."

Snake continued, "Shirley was direct and didn't pull any punches, in contrast to what I saw as Coach's mostly non-confrontational style and congeniality. In that car, she was the boss. In all the time I knew him, Coach never scared me. But Shirley did."

Snake is one of the few athletes in Carleton history (maybe the only one) to take his oral comps while wearing his game-day uniform. At Carleton, comprehensive exams or "Comps" are a requirement for all seniors; comps are a capstone project in the student's major, and can take the form of a written or oral exam, a research paper, a creative performance, etc. Snake remembered: "We only went 3-15 my senior season, losing a couple heartbreakers. Two of the three wins happened the same day, against Macalester. I pitched in the first game, had a solid complete game outing and we won, 2-1.

My oral comps were scheduled for the same day. I finished pitching and then headed up the hill to Leighton Hall and gave my presentation, 'On the Character of Octavian,' to the Classics Department while in my baseball uniform and cleats. The department chair, David Porter, had apparently played infield at Yale in his younger days. He kind of chuckled at my attire and not only did I get my first and only win of the season, but I passed my oral comps. After the presentation, I headed back down to the field hoping to catch the end of the second game. We started Randy Beller at pitcher. We were not expecting a win, but when I got back to the field, the game was over and Randy 'Doc' Beller had pitched a complete game shutout, winning 1-0. Baseball is a funny game." It is indeed.

Sully had this thing he called the "Mental Chart." Players on the bench had different jobs to do, some charting pitches, some trying to steal the opposing team's signs, and one guy would keep the Mental Chart, noting when someone made a smart or dumb play on the diamond, such as hitting behind the runner, missing the cutoff man, etc. On one particular day, Jon Darby was keeping the Mental Chart. On a lark, he gave a mental minus to left fielder Bruce Grench for "stealing Christmas." (For those from the younger generation, *How the Grinch Stole Christmas!* was a children's holiday classic, written and illustrated by Dr. Seuss and first published in 1957.) Darbs said, "After the game Sully ran through the Mental Chart with the entire team, noting who got mental pluses and minuses. When he got to Grench's name, he said 'Bruce gets a minus for stealing Christmas.' He never paused and went on to

the next name on the list. None of us were sure if he even noticed the joke."
Hmmm.

The players all knew that Sully wanted to start practice on time. He created
an environment where the precise starting time was a unique 3:29, not 3:30.
Brent Siegel recalled, "During baseball one year he let us know he was unhappy about our showing up for practice on time. Whenever we would show
up (a few minutes late) he would say, 'Where the hell have you guys been?!'
He stated that being on time for baseball should be easy compared to football
– where we were on time always – since for baseball getting dressed for practice was so much easier than football because all we needed for baseball were
cleats, a cap, and a jockstrap.

So, the next day, we all showed up on time and when Coach walked out
to the field we were all wearing *just* cleats, caps and jockstraps. Coach laughed
as hard as the rest of us."

Someone took a photo of those guys, which is still in circulation. It is
quite the team picture! Apparently, this ritual became an annual tradition for
many years with subsequent Knight baseball teams. They would show up
one day each season in cleats, caps and jocks, then proudly take their regular
pre-practice jog around the entire baseball field, making sure that everyone
who drove by on old Highway 19 got a good look at their jiggling fannies.

One year, on one of the previously mentioned southern road trips, the Knights
found themselves in a southern state which shall remain nameless, and they
stopped at a small college, which shall also remain nameless. Sully always
arranged the logistics for these trips, and he strove to save a buck wherever he
could, ever the good steward of Carleton's scarce financial resources.

The boys were going to play a double header starting the next morning,
so they needed a place nearby to bed down for the night. For purposes of this

story, we will call this school Whatsamatta U. Sully led the team into Whatsamatta U's gymnasium, then into their locker room, then into a dank, windowless room off the locker room, that happened to contain a whole bunch of bunk beds. "Here you go guys. Get your rest. See you in the morning," he told them. Sully and Shirley then headed off to the local Holiday Inn.

The guys looked at each other, scratched their heads, then did what any energetic, enterprising band of young athletes would do in just such a situation: they picked the men among them who were of age and sent them off to buy beer which, after quite a search, they succeeded in doing. They were not aware that the school resided in a dry county.

The boys had barely cracked the first cans of golden nectar when, WHAM, they were accosted by the college's head of security. He was described by one of the players later as being, "a stereotypical Southern law-enforcement type." If you ever watched the TV show, *Dukes of Hazzard*, you know what he was talking about.

The pot-bellied gentleman seized their beer and, with his partner, proceeded to the restroom where he gleefully poured all of it down the drain. The guys tried not to cry. He warned them, in his slow drawl, "Fellas, I'm gonna hafta let your coach know about this. Who is he and where's he stayin'?" He got Sully's contact info and proceeded to an office with a phone. Bob Bradovich simply could not pass up the opportunity. This was gonna be priceless.

"Excuse me sir, would you mind if I and a couple of the other guys listen in on your call with our coach?"

"Naw, come on. You boys are up shit's creek and in a whole heepa trouble."

Brado wasn't so sure. He thought to himself, "We'll see."

They gathered around the phone. Ring, ring.

"Coach Sullivan?"

"Yeah."

"This here is Buford T. Foghorn [fictional name] over at Whatsamatta U. Yeah. I'm head of the security detail over here, Coach, and I'm with your boys and, well, we got us a problem."

"Goddammit! What did they do?"

"Well, they been drinkin' Coach."

Pause.

"Yeah? What else?"

"Well, like I said, they been drinkin'."

Long pause.

"Did they break anything?"

"No."

"Did they steal anything?"

"No."

"WERE THERE ANY WOMEN INVOLVED?!"

"No."

"Then what the hell's the problem?!"

"Well, they been drinkin' Coach, and this here's a dry campus in a dry county."

"W'hell, when they're back on our campus, that's all they do!"

The next day, there was no mention of the previous evening's "incident." Brado reflected later, "You know, the moral of that story is that Sully always had our back. He really did."

Later, Coach admitted to the team, "You guys think you were upset we were in a dry county. Shirley was livid. No cocktail hour. I caught hell for that."

CHAPTER 15

Endgame to Checkmate

"I haven't figured out football and I never will. I accept that. Still, I get up every day and chase perfection, even though I know it's unattainable."

BILL BELICHICK

"There are no gray areas in this business here. Your earnings aren't kind of up, and your quarterly reports don't kind of look better. You either won or you lost."

BILL PARCELS

The 1993 Knights went 6-4. That was, unfortunately, the last winning season of Coach Sullivan's Carleton career. The luster of the MIAC championship in '92 helped bring in a healthy total of 27 freshmen recruits the next year. In the recruiting process, Sully acknowledged the challenges he faced but made a point of focusing on the positive: "It always seems more difficult for a school like Carleton, with a strong academic reputation that supersedes all else, that athletics and football in particular can also provide excellence…

One of the things that I always try to impress upon recruits - and anyone else who will listen – is the great tradition that we have here at Carleton. While not as impressive from a win-loss standpoint as St. John's or St. Thomas, Carleton football history is steeped in solid and, for the most part, winning traditions."

Among the group that joined the squad in '93 was Scott Klein, from Apple Valley, Minnesota, who went on to a three-time All-MIAC and C-Club Hall of Fame career. Scott was a four-year starter as the hybrid linebacker/rover in the Bear defense, and before he was done, he set the school record for tackles. Matt Hoffman teamed up with Klein at linebacker, and also became one of Sully's best ever. The 1993 team was superb on offense and young on defense, which made for an interesting season.

There were a couple of highlight games, and several career records were set by the end of the campaign. Both the Knights and the Oles went into the annual battle for the Goat Trophy at 3-2 overall, 2-2 in the MIAC. The game turned into a track meet that, Sully recalled, "would prove to be a nightmare for defensive coordinators, as neither team could stop the other and whomever had the ball last would win... 1,140 yards of total offense was registered between the two squads." The lead went back and forth four times before the Knights poured on the gas in the fourth quarter with three touchdowns and ended up prevailing, 51-48. Ryan Beckers filled in for an injured Ted Kluender at QB and earned MIAC Player of the Week honors with five TD passes. The *Carletonian* proclaimed that the game was "enacted and climaxed in epic fashion."

In the season finale at Laird, the Knights won in a comeback thriller, 35-30, for their seventh victory in the last nine tries over Gustavus. The game represented the 11th straight home win for the boys in maize and blue, and clinched their eighth upper-division MIAC finish in the last nine seasons.

The '93 Knights were prolific offensively, finishing 10th in DIII with 443 yards of total offense and 19th overall with 246 passing yards per game. Adam Henry ended his stellar career as Carleton's all-time leading rusher with 3,482 yards. At the time of his graduation, he also held the MIAC career record for all-purpose career offense with 5,620 yards. Despite missing four games with injury, Ted Kluender finished his career as the all-time school leader with 50 TD passes and 5,058 passing yards, records that have since been broken. Sully summarized, "This was to be the last winning season for a long time and one which marked the end of yet another great era for Carleton football." From 1985 to 1993, the Knights won 55 football games, one of the most outstanding runs in school history. Nevertheless, continued success in 1994 and beyond would require a rebuild, and years of frustration and disappointment followed.

In 1994, 24 freshmen committed to play for Sully. A key future star among them was Skye Flanagan, who hurt himself in the pre-season and missed the entire year. He would recover fully and go on to become one of Sully's most excellent running backs.

Carleton, still a young team, finished the season 3-7. They dropped the opener, 36-31 to Cornell of Iowa, snapping their 11-game winning streak at Laird. The next week, St. Thomas whipped the Knights, 19-0. The last time the boys had been shut out was 1983. They went to 0-3 in a tight game against Gustavus but finally got into the win column in week four against Macalester, 38-19. Perhaps the best game of the year came against the Oles at Laird, with 5,500 fans in attendance. The Knights amassed more than 500 yards of offense in defeating Olaf, 18-6. The Johnnies, who would win the MIAC that year, wiped the floor with our guys once again, 63-20. The Knights went into the Augsburg contest at 2-6, with the Auggies fielding a strong squad. In the most thrilling game of the year, Carleton eked out a one-point victory, 28-27, for their final win of a disappointing season.

Chris French had a great year at fullback, rushing for 937 yards and scoring 10 touchdowns. But turnovers hurt, with Carleton's quarterbacks throwing a combined 29 interceptions on the season. Sully lamented, "The interception bugaboo would haunt us for several seasons." He summed up the frustration they all felt: "Statistically, the Knights gave up 32 points per game and only averaged 19 of their own. This pretty much told the story of the season."

The 1995 season became something of a weird repeat of '94. Again, exactly 24 freshmen showed up for camp and again, the team's record ended up disheartening 3-7. Andy Quist, who hailed from Alexandria, Minnesota, joined the team and developed into one of Sully's most versatile players ever. French hurt himself early in the year, then sat out with the goal of returning in 1996.

The team's three victories came against Gustavus in the home opener, 29-21; Macalester, 36-13; and the Oles. The Olaf game, as it had been so many times in the fabled 73-year rivalry, was once again the highlight of the season. The Knights led, 14-0, at the half but the Oles came storming back to take a one-point lead, 15-14, with 3:35 remaining. Carleton mounted a dramatic 12-play, 86-yard touchdown drive to win, 21-15. The Knights put up 441 yards of offense, with QB C.G. Shoap passing for 300 yards. Sully concluded, "This win would go down with the '81, '85, and '93 games as one of the top St. Olaf games for me as coach. All were classics and memorable for everyone involved."

Despite the intense disappointment of not winning another game for the remainder of the year, some of the best football athletes ever to don the maize and blue played for Sully and were brilliant in '95. Al Stier was the rare three-sport athlete at Carleton (basketball and track were his other sports), and he contributed significantly on both sides of the ball. Sully said, "Al was one of the best athletes I had ever been around." Pat Rowan, one of Sully's three all-time best defensive tackles, made first-team All-MIAC. Scott Klein was also a first-team All-MIAC performer. He was Sully's ferocious hybrid linebacker who started all four years and became the school's all-time leading tackler. Matt Hoffman also excelled at linebacker.

The 1996 season represented something of a rebound year, as the Knights finished 5-5 for their last upper division MIAC finish in a long time. Recruiting was down, with only 14 freshmen reporting to camp. One of those recruits was Paul Kane, who went on to an outstanding career as one of Sully's best at offensive guard. It was an exciting season, but also discouraging in that the team lost two games by one point and another in overtime. As one might expect with a .500 team, while the Knights' offense generated an impressive 29 points per game, an inexperienced and porous defense gave up 28 points per game.

The season began on a hopeful note with an opening game victory at Laird over Lawrence, 33-15. Skye Flanagan flashed his skills with 151 rushing yards and a pair of TDs. The next game represented the first Knights' shutout since 1992, as they blanked Macalester, 22-0. Then came a string of heartbreaking defeats, several of them narrow, commencing with a 28-27 loss to the Royals of Bethel. The Johnnies put their usual thumping on the Knights, 64-7, in an embarrassing rout. A Homecoming win over Augsburg, 43-36, raised spirits. Flanagan and Chris French combined for over 200 yards rushing. But a crushing overtime loss the next week, 20-14 to Hamline caused our boys to wonder whether they were "snakebit" for the season.

The high point of the year - or low point, depending on your perspective - came in a historic contest at Laird against St. Thomas. Despite generating an astounding 760 yards of total offense and scoring 54 points, the Knights still fell just short one more time against the hated Tommies, 55-54. The total offense and scoring numbers for Carleton both represented DIII records for a losing team. Carleton would have won with a gutsy decision to go for a two-point conversion with 55 seconds remaining in the game, but the try failed. Sully said after the game, "It had been a memorable day, one which would stay in the record books for years, and to come up short by one point after the same thing happened the week before at Bethel was tough to take."

A decisive win over the Oles, 42-9, was the 10th win in the last 11 games against the cross-town nemesis. The Knights finally experienced some luck on Parents Day at Laird with a close 17-14 win over Gustavus. In the final game of the year at the Metrodome, the whole thing ended on a fittingly disappointing note with a 36-26 loss to the Cobbers of Concordia.

Despite it all, when the campaign was over, Sully still believed that this team was one of the best ones he had ever coached at Carleton. The Knights finished only 18 points away from a 9-1 season, with all the close losses. Sully concluded, "It was déjà vu all over again, much as the '90 season had gone (also a 5-5 finish) with four close games that went the wrong way. This was one of the best teams we ever had, the last team to date that has challenged the top teams."

The final four years of Coach Sullivan's tenure at Carleton did not go well. In the spring of 1997, the entire college community was saddened to learn of the death of Tom Nielson. Sully remembered his talented, loyal assistant and dear friend: "Tom Nielson, father of Tim and John and an assistant football coach with me at Carleton from '88 to '93, died of a heart attack in May of 1997 in Montana. Tom had also coached baseball here during those years and had led us to the MIAC baseball title in '91. Tom was one of my best friends. In 2002 head coach Chris Brann began awarding a 'Rookie of the Year' award to the best freshman player. This award was named the 'Tom Nielson Award' in honor of Tom."

Hopes were high in '97 with the arrival of 30 freshman recruits, Sully's biggest class ever. Among that group were four players who would make Sully's all-time list: Geoff Thurk and J.J. Franz were outstanding defensive ends; Josh Schroeder was a defensive back who also starred in baseball; and Dan Reider was a fine all-around player at receiver and running back, who also specialized in electrifying punt and kick returns.

The Knights only recorded two wins all year. They beat Lawrence in Appleton, Wisconsin, 29-19 in the opener and in the very next game defeated Macalester in St. Paul, 21-3. After that, the proverbial wheels fell off, and they finished the season a depressing 2-8. Sully struggled to find answers: "What happened? There are several theories and ideas... Andy Quist, the outstanding athlete who [played so many roles for us] was injured in practice after the first game and was out for the season... The second theory advanced was that we had our collective heart broken by the incredible close losses from the year before... a few of the seniors who had great junior years came back out of shape... and finally, the turnover ratio was almost unbelievable as we probably led the nation with a -31 on the season..."

There was one high point as a kind of coda to an otherwise unsuccessful season. Yogi Reppmann was a German professor at Carleton, and he had suggested to Coach over winter break that the team take a trip to Germany, which he would host. Sully liked the idea, floated it with the administration, and the trip was on. The players paid their own way, but the costs were reasonable, and 30 guys chose to participate. They traveled to Germany over spring break in March of 1998.

A great time was had by all. They played two football games, against German teams that were more enthusiastic than skilled. The Knights won both contests handily. They also had an opportunity to sightsee throughout Northern Germany, eat good food and drink German beer, as well as get to know the incredibly interesting and kind German people whom they met along the way. Sully said, "The Germans were perfect hosts, a sportsmanlike group, and Yogi Reppmann was the perfect guide. It was a very positive experience for everyone."

Among the 28 recruits who showed up to play ball in 1998 was an outstanding linebacker and future Sully all-star, Scott O'Reilly. But high hopes that this team would fare better than the '97 squad were soon dashed. Sully explained, "This was a good football team with a great attitude and work ethic and the team would play much better football overall than it did in '97 and deserved a better fate than the 2-8 season it was dealt. Four close losses, all by less than a touchdown, were the difference. The Knights had forgotten how to win, but they had not forgotten how to compete in the MIAC." The only two victories on the season were against Northwestern of St. Paul, 31-14, in the opener, and Macalester at Homecoming, 34-7. The game against Mac was the first official "Brain Game," and the two schools would forever going forward compete for the "Book of Knowledge." The Knights now had a second trophy to play for each season, along with the Goat Trophy for bragging rights against the Oles.

By the next year, Sully had arrived at one of the most important decisions of his career: "I had made up my mind during the summer of 1999 that the 2000 season would be my last. Health issues, the desire to spend more time with my wife, and the recent losing had taken its toll... I told only the Athletic Director and the President of my plan as I did not want to disrupt the seasons in any way. The plan was to announce the formal retirement after mid-season in 2000, which is exactly the way it went down."

Regarding his health, Coach had developed an irregular heartbeat, also known as atrial fibrillation, and been hospitalized overnight twice in recent years after losses to St. Olaf. In 2002, he had a pacemaker surgically installed. Sully also admitted many years later another reason that he believed it was time to be done: the newfangled digital technology around reviewing game action sort of baffled him; it wasn't like the old days when he sat for hours in John Gagliardi's living room studying film with Gags, using a good old-fashioned film projector. Sometimes, technology is not our friend.

Sully was also under pressure to "get the monkey off my back" and win his 100th game at Carleton, which finally happened in the first contest of the '99 season. That milestone achievement, against Northwestern in the opener, 21-14, along with a Homecoming victory over Hamline, 16-13, were the only two wins of the year. For the third consecutive season, the Knights finished at 2-8.

Sully said of his grand finale in 2000, "I was convinced that this, my final season, would be a successful one on the field of play." But alas, it was not to be: "While we would improve in many areas and prove to be competitive for three quarters of every game, we always seemed to have a poor performance in one quarter which would make the difference. We continued to play hard, but we had obviously forgotten how to win, as we slipped to 1-9 overall and 1-8 in league play." In the lone victory of the season, the Knights secured the Book of Knowledge, defeating Macalester in St. Paul, 27-14.

After the October 28 game in Moorhead against the Cobbers (a 38-14 loss), Sully announced his retirement to the team. It was an emotional moment. He remembered, "There were some tears and hugs all around as it was one of the most difficult announcements I ever had to make. I loved football, coaching, the players, the school – everything – but the time was right."

Coach Sullivan's retirement became "official" in December of 2000, but he continued to teach in the P.E. Department, as he had always done, through the winter term (among other subjects that Sully taught over the years were classroom courses on football and coaching theory, and experiential courses such as weightlifting, orienteering, and skiing; when he took the students skiing at a nearby resort called Welch Village, he paid for their lift tickets, sent them on their way to ski, and then, "went to the chalet, relaxed and had my lunch.") He was done at Carleton by March of 2001. It had been a great run.

Sully was particularly touched by the words of Carleton President Stephen Lewis who, ironically, announced his own retirement 48 hours after Sully announced his. Lewis said, "Bob Sullivan's teams often have shown electrifying offense, but I'll think of the character they've shown and the ability to win big games, to be competitive with much bigger teams and to come from behind to win. Hundreds of young men have had a great experience because of Bob's leadership, and we will miss him enormously."

When it was all over, many years later, Sully stated the obvious: "If I hadn't coached those last four years at Carleton, had retired in 1996, I would have had a helluva better won-loss record and winning percentage than I did." For a man who hated losing as much as Sully did, it was all very tough to take. Indeed, had he cut things off at the end of the '96 season he would have achieved a career record of 95-81, for a very respectable .540 winning percentage. But he stuck it out and ended his still legendary career with a record 102 wins and 114 losses (also a record), for a .472 winning percentage. Lots of things can happen, both good and bad, over a 22-year time span.

As always, Sully chose to focus on the positive. He was the winningest coach in Carleton football history, by an extremely large margin. In his era, he had coached six first-team All-Americans, ten honorable mention All-Americans, and 85 All-Conference athletes. Oh, and let's not forget the two Rhodes Scholars (Mike Gillette, '81, and Paul Vaaler, '83). Coach was easily as proud of those two guys as he was of any of the others.

Bubba Sullivan once researched a comparison of Carleton's football program under his dad's leadership against other top academic schools at the DI level that played in extremely competitive conferences. From 1979 to 2000, among Stanford and Cal-Berkely in the Pac 10, Northwestern in the Big Ten, Rice in the Southwest Conference, Vanderbilt in the SEC, and Duke in the ACC, only Stanford had a better football winning percentage than the Knights of Carleton College. That's impressive company.

Sully always had the gift of perspective. When he won his 100th game, he said, "It feels like I've never actually worked in my life. I don't know how all these people do it: getting up and working to make a living. I've been able to go out and do what I want to do each day, and loving it… To me, what I really take pride in when I think of the 100 victories, is that they all came at a school known for academics and prestige… What's kept me going here is the type of student-athlete I get to work with. They're fun to coach, they're all bright and I've never had any problems that coaches in DI and DII have to deal with… Carleton football has never been boring, we may not always win, but we're always fun to watch."

A group of influential football alums pushed for Bubba Sullivan to take the head coaching position at Carleton once his dad was done. His coaching record and his pedigree were, of course, superb. Bubba thought about it seriously. He acknowledged, "There were some sleepless nights." But in the end, he decided that while he loved football, his father was in love with football, and there was a difference. "I decided I really liked the balance I had as a high school coach who also very much enjoyed the teaching aspect of my job. If you want to coach successfully at the collegiate level, you have to be all in. I wasn't prepared to make that sacrifice, and so I passed on the opportunity. I occasionally think about how my career would have been different, but I don't have any regrets."

Carleton football struggled for many years to "remember how to win again" after Coach Sullivan left. The College hired Chris Brann to replace Sully. Brann had coached as a defensive assistant at Marietta College of Ohio, Robert Morris in Pennsylvania, Rochester University in New York, and the University of Chicago. Brann's record with the Knights from 2001 to 2005 was 9-41. He was replaced by Kurt Ramler in 2006. Ramler had been a star player and one in a long line of terrific QBs at St. John's. He had coached as an assistant for the Johnnies, and also at Wagner College and Hamilton College, both in New York.

Ramler had a bit more success, coaching the Knights to a 22-38 record from '06 to 2011. In 2008 he was MIAC Coach of the Year after leading the boys to a 7-3 record, the first winning season since 1993.

In January 2012, Ramler resigned, and Carleton hired Bob Pagel to replace him, first on an interim basis and then as head coach. He had been a Knights defensive assistant for the past seven seasons. During Pagel's tenure, the boys continued their losing ways, with an overall record of 12-48 and 6-42 in the MIAC from '12 to 2017.

When the commanding and charismatic figure that is Tom Journell first came to campus in 2018 as Carleton's 18th head football coach, his situation closely resembled the one Sully stepped into in 1979. The Knights had won just two games in the three seasons prior to Journell's arrival. He faced a rebuilding project of monumental proportions. As Mark Twain observed, "History does not repeat itself, but it rhymes." Once more, a larger-than-life personality would work hard to ensure the phoenix that was the Carleton football program would rise again from the ashes.

Coach Journell brought 32 years of coaching experience, having been a head coach at both UW-Stevens Point and Elmhurst College in Illinois. He says that he was "recruited" to come to Carleton by his son Mack, who was one of the best wide receivers in Carleton history and continued to thrive under his dad's leadership.

Coach J has done a magnificent job, under incredibly difficult circumstances, to build a winning program. Through sheer willpower he has made it happen. At the conclusion of the 2024 season, he owned a career record of 33-27 at Carleton, which makes him the first coach with a winning record since Warren Beson, who was 21-7-2 when he tragically passed away in 1959. From 2021 to 2024, Coach J's young warriors won 26 games. Only one other group of Carleton seniors ever won more games than the '24 seniors. Those were the Bob Sullivan coached boys who played from 1986 to 1989, winning 27 games during that span.

Coach Journell has a phrase that he repeats: "Keep Stackin.'" It means strive to get better every day, in everything you do. Sounds familiar. Carleton Knight football fans everywhere wish Coach J continued good luck in his determined pursuit of excellence. Keep Stackin' brother. Go Knights!

CHAPTER 16

Bubba & the Northfield Raiders

"Many shall run to and fro, and knowledge shall be increased."

DANIEL 12:4

"Only three things can happen when you throw the ball and two of them are bad."

WOODY HAYES, DARRELL ROYAL, BO SCHEMBECHLER AND COUNTLESS OTHER FOOTBALL COACHES SINCE THE FIRST LEGAL FORWARD PASS WAS THROWN IN 1906

To observe Bubba Sullivan tenderly wrap a warm blanket around the old man's shoulders, then steadily hold an umbrella over his head on a cold, nasty, rainy game day Saturday at Bob Sullivan Field, Laird Stadium, is to bear quiet witness to a devoted son's undying, eternal love and respect for his father.

Like his father, who developed pyloric stenosis as an infant, Bubba Sullivan had challenges from the very beginning. When he was born in June of 1966, he was a preemie baby. He had arrived four weeks early, and he only weighed between three and four pounds at birth. He spent three-and-one-half weeks in an incubator. Like his father, he was a fighter who survived and grew up to thrive.

His given name is Bob Theodore. His father nicknamed him "Bubba" when he was around two years old in honor of Bubba Smith, who was an All-American defensive lineman at Michigan State. Big Bubba stood 6'7" tall and weighed 265 pounds, massive dimensions for that era. He went on to an illustrious Hall of Fame career in the NFL. Father Bob thought the contrast between gigantic Bubba Smith and tiny Bob Sullivan was notable and worthy of the nickname. The moniker stuck.

When he was three, the family was living in Brooklyn Park and Bubba was just down the block playing with the local gang of kids. A bit later, the Sullivans got a knock and the door and one of the neighborhood moms asked if they knew where the Smith family lived. "No, we haven't heard of them," the Sullivans said. "Hmm," the woman responded, "We have a little boy here who says his name is Bubba Smith and we are trying to help him get home." "We'll take him," said Bob and Shirley with a smile.

Also like his father, Bubba was a fine multi-sport athlete as a schoolboy and chose St. John's University for college. Like his father, he did not play collegiate football. Like his father, he graduated with an English degree and then became a teacher and head football coach at the high school level, right off the bat. Finally, like his father, he had a long and successful career as a head football coach.

Bubba had been exposed to football at an early age. He followed his dad around the Cooper practice field as a tot. By the time the family moved to Northfield, adolescent Bubba was a full-fledged ball boy for the Carleton Knights, experiencing the sights and sounds of a football program up close. It was at this point that he considered coaching as a possible career. Bubba graduated from Northfield High School in 1985. He lettered nine times in football, hockey and baseball, captaining the hockey and baseball teams and earning All-Conference honors in both sports. As a football quarterback and defensive back, he broke his arm in the third game of his senior season and, from there, just looked forward to focusing on hockey.

Jack McNamara was the head hockey coach, and he had a significant impact on Bubba, who recalled, "He was a great coach; first of all, he made hockey fun, but he was also tough and a disciplinarian who was a former military policeman. He praised us when we did things right and when we didn't, we were corrected. We just really loved playing for him." The idea of enjoying sports while at the same time striving to excel stuck with Bubba.

When it came time for Bubba to choose a college, though he was accepted for admission, he passed on Carleton. "I was a hockey player, and Carleton did not then and doesn't now have a varsity hockey program," he said. "So, I decided to go to St. Johns [his older brother Tim had quarterbacked the Johnny football team] where I ended up playing hockey all four years." He graduated in 1989 after winning four letters and captaining the team, in addition to receiving academic honors.

Bubba was looking for an opportunity to teach English and, hopefully, coach hockey at the prep level. He cast a wide net but, serendipitously, an opening came up for a teaching role and a head coaching position at his alma mater, Northfield High School. But the head coaching job was for the football team. He jumped at the chance.

At the time, Bubba held a summer job that, among other responsibilities, involved mowing the grass on the football field at NHS. He was in mid-mow, stopped, wiped the sweat off his brow, donned a coat and tie, went inside the school for his job interview, got back into his work attire, then hopped on the machine and continued cutting the grass. While he was doing that, Athletic Director Kevin Merkle (who had also been Bubba's head football coach at NHS and would now become an assistant working for him for the next several years), walked out and told him, "Well, you got the job." That fall, Bubba was on the same field, this time with a whistle and playbook in hand and a football team that desperately needed his leadership.

Bubba was the head coach at Northfield for 32 years, stepping down in 2020. He achieved a career record of 208-134, for a .608 winning percentage. During that span, the Raiders won 10 conference titles, 11 section championships, were the state runner-up four times, and won a state title in 1997. Bubba coached more the 150 athletes who went on to play college football (including a number who played for his dad at Carleton). Two of his players, the Setterstrom brothers, Mark and Chad, went on to play in the NFL. Bubba was the Minnesota Football Coaches Association Coach of the Year in 1997, and he is a member of the MFCA's Hall of Fame (as is his father).

Bubba has won widespread admiration and praise for his role over three-plus decades as a teacher and coach who positively influenced the lives of thousands of kids, regular students as well as athletes. He continues in that role as of this writing. Early in his tenure, his mom Shirley suggested he could run successfully for mayor of Northfield. She said, "It is a cliché, but he is one of the nicest people you will meet. I'm so happy for him, because he loves teaching too, not just the coaching." (You can always count on your mom to say good and positive things, but Shirley was right: Bubba Sullivan is indeed a wonderful gentleman who is an incredibly nice guy.)

In an article from the Northfield News, upon the occasion of Bubba's 25th anniversary as head football coach in 2013, Northfield High School activities director Tom Graupman recalled, "I remember when he first came. We were like 'Bubba? That young? [he was 23 years old] Looking back, talk about hitting the jackpot… He's a model citizen. A role model. We're lucky to have kept him this long, and we're hoping to keep him to retirement. We're just blessed he's back in the community… He's done so many significant things."

Just as Bob Sullivan struggled over several dismal seasons in his first job at Cooper to create a positive culture and build a winning team, the beginning of the journey for Bubba was not easy either. He started by taking his dad's Carleton playbook, whiting out "Carleton" on the front cover and penciling in "Northfield." He cut out plays he thought his boys couldn't run, many of them passing plays.

Even with significant help and support from his older, established assistant coaches – guys who had coached Bubba just a few years earlier - the first two seasons were a struggle. The Raiders won two games in Bubba's inaugural season. In year two they regressed, and in the final game of a winless season, the Raiders were pummeled by Lakeville South 65-0. A group of underclassmen approached Bubba after the game and promised him they would never be beaten like that again. Bubba said, "We were in turnaround mode, just as my dad was, first at Cooper and then at Carleton. I adopted and implemented Bob's psychology of winning philosophy. I also learned from his example and did not do a lot of screaming and hollering; we were gonna be as positive as we could. My challenge was to get the kids to think like winners before we actually were winners."

The next year things got better. A critical factor was an intense focus on getting stronger. "What really turned us around, quite frankly, was the weight room," Bubba recalled. "This was a key for us in the '90s. We got to the point where we ran the ball really well because we were just stronger than the opposition. We pounded the football down people's throats because we could." Offensively, Bubba used a twin veer attack like his father but also ran out of the old Wing-T formation as well. On defense, it was a 50 read and 50 slide (see Chapter 9), just as Bob had run successfully at Carleton.

In 1991, the Raiders defeated a very tough Holy Angels team and top-ranked Hutchinson, both milestone victories. At homecoming, they battled the same Lakeville South team that had throttled them the previous year to a 0-0 score at the end of regulation, only to lose 3-0 in overtime. Assistant coach Jeff Heckroth summed up what happened next: "From there, we got good. We got really good." During the next decade the Raiders won Section titles in five straight seasons from 1993-1997. They were twice state runners-up and finally achieved the dream in capturing the Class 4A state championship in '97. There were five more state tourney appearances in the 2000s and another title game runner-up finish in 2008.

By that time, a very capable offensive coordinator had joined Bubba's staff. His name was Bob Sullivan. Sully just plain missed football and coaching in the two empty years after his retirement from Carleton in 2000. "I was lost," he admitted. He and Bubba talked, and the deal was done. What else could Bubba do? In the mid-'90s he reflected on his dad's legacy: "I know I'm biased, but I think he is one of the greatest coaches I have ever met or seen coach." Once he joined the staff, Bob in turn raved about his son, "It's just been great coaching with Bubba; he's done a fabulous job with the program."

Mutual admiration aside, respect for another coach's experience and talent does not necessarily translate into agreement on football philosophy and schemes. Head coaches need to make decisions, and when an assistant expresses a different thought, he is invariably overruled. A headline from a 2007 publication called Northfield Portraits announced: "Sullivans are working side by side." The article explained the reality of the dynamic: "It's not very often that a father takes orders from his son, but when it comes to high school football, that's exactly the situation for the coaching duo of Bob and Bubba Sullivan."

Specifically, Bob tended to want to throw the football; Bubba was generally content to play the safe odds and stay on the ground. Northfield Portraits continued: "Bob was legendary at Carleton for having a run-and-gun aerial attack, while Bubba is known in Northfield as a fairly conservative coach who sticks to the running game." Bob never questioned authority, nor did he ever get too bent out of shape. "It's a running joke," he said; "His brother Tim and I call him 'Ground Chuck' after Chuck Knox [an NFL coach who adored the running game]. He doesn't like to throw."

Tim Sullivan swears there was at least one instance on a game day Friday when the offensive coordinator (Bob Sullivan) called a pass play from the box up above to the head coach (Bubba Sullivan) down on the field. It was one of the old man's all-time most effective passes, a true favorite, and was deeply embedded in his mind. He had relied on it in the clutch for years. The terse response from the head coach went back up to the box: "Hey guess what? I don't wanna run that play, and we're not gonna run that play, for the primary reason that IT'S NOT EVEN IN OUR PLAYBOOK!"

The run versus pass difference of opinion, as it went between father and son, was actually quite amusing, and reminiscent of the old "tastes great – less filling" Miller Lite beer commercials from years ago (which starred Bubba Smith, incidentally, among other football luminaries like Dick Butkus,

Paul Hornung and John Madden). It's one of those arguments that will probably never be fully settled. But the back and forth was really fun.

In Bubba's defense, the reality was more nuanced. Compared to college, there is a dearth of skill position high school athletes. "We obviously didn't get to recruit, we just had to play with whoever showed up. The number of kids at that level who can throw and catch with great ability is not that many; it doesn't happen very often." He was never entirely against the idea of passing the ball, he just chose to do what worked. Bubba's philosophy evolved out of practical experience. Like his dad, in an ideal world he would have executed a balanced attack. "My initial instinct was that we would run the ball 60 percent of the time and throw 40 percent. But what I found out was that the 40 percent just was not as productive."

Nevertheless, the Raiders did throw the ball. During the '90s when they were at their best, a typical game would result in 250 rushing and 100 passing yards, on six completions in eight attempts. Often, two or three of those passing plays, because they succeeded in surprising the opposition, would result in touchdowns. In addition, 15 of the top 20 NHS career passing yardage leaders were QBs who played for Bubba. While there was certainly no aerial circus happening under Friday night lights at Northfield High during the Bubba Sullivan era, he did pass the ball, but only strategically and selectively. Like any good coach, he matched the game plan to his personnel. And he won football games.

During their cherished time coaching together, the Sullivans experienced their ups and downs; some seasons were more successful than others. They got to a state championship game in 2008, and they also endured a pandemic that caused high school sports to be shut down everywhere. On balance, they went out as winners, and it was an unforgettable experience for both.

In looking back, Bob said, "It was incredibly enjoyable, fun and easy." His respect for and pride in his son as a coach is immense. "Bubba was just an ideal high school football coach. He was fair, steady and consistent. Each player was a valued member of the team, he did not play favorites. His players did not call him Coach, they just called him Bubba. There was no yelling, and his focus was not exclusively on winning. He loved to win, for sure, but he also wanted the experience to be fun for everyone. There was an emphasis on enjoyment and positivity, not just winning. Parents were delighted to have Bubba as their son's coach."

CHAPTER 17

MAN OF LETTERS

Knights of the Gridiron

"I sincerely hope people will appreciate and enjoy the book. It is part history, large part autobiography, part humor, part anecdotal, and part love affair with the game of football. Above all, it is about Carleton College football – a unique, positive and distinct experience for the wonderful and diverse young men who contributed to and were indeed the essence of Carleton football."

FROM THE FORWARD TO *KNIGHTS OF THE GRIDIRON*, BY BOB SULLIVAN

In 2004, Coach Sullivan decided to write a book about the history of Carleton football. Thus was born, *Knights of the Gridiron: A History of Carleton College Football, 1883-2005*. The two-year-long process of research and writing finally afforded Coach the opportunity to utilize his undergrad and master's-level education in English, as well as to demonstrate his skills as a wordsmith and express his lifelong love of language. He enjoyed the journey immensely.

What it takes to write a book is the discipline to sit down every day and write until there is a book. Not many people want to do it. Not many people can do it.

Sully kept his process simple. The College encouraged him in the effort and gave him office space in the form of a tiny, windowless room in the bowels of Goodsell Observatory, which was built in 1885, houses three historic telescopes, and used to be the home of Carleton's astronomy department.

Sully started by spending endless hours scouring records and photographs in the Carleton Archives, as well as his own treasure-trove of football-related materials. Once he gathered his data, Shirley would drop him off four or five days a week at Goodsell and he would spend four hours in the morning typing his manuscript. He continued to work in the fall even as he spent his afternoons helping Bubba coach the NHS Raiders.

It takes a village to produce a book. Sully appreciated the efforts of Jon "Whitey" Nicholson, who held many roles – including Admissions Director - in his 34-year career at Carleton, and Mike Kowalewski, English professor, as his proofreaders. Carleton's Archivist, Eric Hilleman, and Sports Information Director Eric Siger were tremendously helpful. Megan Ward and Ben Cooperider were Carleton students who greatly aided the process. Sully's daughter-in-law, Bubba's spouse, Julie Nikolai Sullivan, did a superb job with the creative design and layout of the book. His grandson Jake Heath provided much-needed technical expertise.

The volume this team produced is not quite a coffee table book at 11.5" by 9" and 186 pages, but it is substantial. *Knights of the Gridiron* is beautifully designed and replete with fascinating black-and-white photos, going back to the very beginnings of the game at Carleton. Unfortunately, the book is no longer in print. Those 600 or so of Sully's Knights who purchased copies almost 20 years ago should hold on to their cherished heirloom.

Sully begins the book with his favorite football poem, written by his long-time friend Ron Stolski, one of the most successful high school football coaches in Minnesota history:

THE BOYS OF AUTUMN

"It is but a game. But such a game.
No matter where it is played or how many view,
Emotions such as joy, disappointment and
Happiness are closer friends now.
Recall crisp fall afternoons when
Your feet were wings, your heart a lion,
Your teammates One,
Go football player… Again."

There are several interesting underlying themes in *Knights*. One is that many things about the great game of football, the men who coach it, and the athletes who play it, haven't changed much.

On the other hand, many things have changed, and dramatically so, since 1883. Football has evolved, and evolved again, many times over the decades. Today's game is more wide open. Offenses have become prolific. Defenses work to adapt. The players today are bigger, stronger, faster, and more athletic. The game is still a dangerous one to play, but not nearly as deadly as it was in 1904, when 18 young men lost their lives on the gridiron. Football has become safer, thankfully. But the bottom line is that football is still football.

One of the best photos in the book is one of the earliest, of the Carleton squad from 1897. By my count there are 29 players and one slender gentleman in a suit and bow tie, who must be the coach – assuming they had one. As was the custom in those days, player uniforms are eclectic rather than identical. Some of the boys wear sweaters, some sport rugby-like jerseys, and two have donned white (student managers?). Most of them have what I assume is a maize-colored "C" sewn onto their front.

One of the men holds a ball that is larger, fatter and rounder than today's football – more like a rugby ball. It would have been fascinating to observe the version of the game that these Knights played. We probably wouldn't much recognize it.

Only two of the players have facial hair, in the form of mustaches; the rest are clean-shaven. The style in those days, apparently, was to wear one's hair longish and parted in the middle. A small handful of the players, however, have their hair parted right or left, and any one of those guys would fit right in as part of Tom Journell's most recent team photo in 2024. No one would have cried out, "Hey, how did that guy from 1897 get into this photo?" Some things never change.

There is always at least one young man on every team who stands out as the iconoclast, the dude who marches to the tune of a different drummer. In this photo, he sits in a casual, laid-back pose, sort of in between the first and second rows. He is non-committal. He is a strapping, good-looking fellow. Very handsome. He looks like a ballplayer; he probably brought the lumber when the time came.

How do we know he is the rebel? His right knee-high sock is plain and dark; his left sock has horizontal stripes; yes, he is rocking mismatching socks. Not a big deal in the grand scheme of the wonderful game of football, but it speaks to a particular outlook and attitude: "I just don't give a shit."

Our version of that teammate in Sully's first season, 82 years after the 1897 photo was snapped, was Mike "Snake" Sullivan, who we introduced in the baseball chapter. Some things never change.

If you ask Sully how the game evolved over the 60 years that he coached, he will say that offenses are more spread out, with a much greater emphasis on the passing game. And the players are bigger. When I played high school football in the mid-1970s, the largest kid on any team that we played all year was probably 6'3" and maybe 265. He was a monster. Today's rosters at any high school with good numbers have probably six or eight guys that size or bigger. The team and individual photos in *Knights* clearly show that the boys have become heftier over time.

Player safety has also gotten better, and there is a particular focus on head injuries now that was non-existent even when I played. I was concussed real good at least three times over my career, twice while returning a punt.

Regarding acceptance of risk in football and, specifically, the job of returning punts, football writer Pat Kirwan said, "Don't ever discount the self-perception of invincibility that is required to play football at any level. If you don't feel invincible, how in the world are you going to go out there to return a punt? Once you start intellectualizing it, thinking that there are 11 guys coming down to blow you up, a rational person would probably say, 'No thanks, I'll pass.' These guys don't pass... they don't willingly ignore the risk; they just don't even consider it."

On the same subject, the authors of *The Hidden Game of Football* said, "The first thought that occurs to us about punt returners is that anyone with enough concentration to focus his attention on a high, turning football while several tons of angry beef are bearing down on him has a great future as a diamond cutter... Well, it's a dirty job, but somebody has to do it; if it were us, though, we'd start calling a fair catch in pregame warmups." With all three of my concussions (none under Sully), goofy and woozy though I may have felt, I immediately went back into the game. There is a reason that football is a young - and sometimes oblivious - man's game.

Fortunately, the equipment is much better now, and rules changes have made what is still a risky sport at least somewhat safer. Photos in the book clearly show the evolution and standardization of uniforms and equipment. The guys in 1897 were not wearing helmets and probably would have been called out as unmanly if they did don protective headgear. Today's helmets are of course mandatory and elaborately designed to reduce the severity of blows to the cranium. With proper concussion protocol, the goal is that the problem will be immediately diagnosed and players will not be sent back into a game with a head injury.

Sully's book is replete not just with photos but with statistics, too. Carleton's football records were current up to the publication date of the book in 2006. There was a lag for many years after that when records were not consistently updated. Thanks to a herculean effort in 2024 involving many hours of research by one of Coach Tom Journell's young warriors, All-MIAC wide receiver Tyler Dimond, the records are now current up to 2025. Ty Di performed a great service for Carlton football history.

The numbers prove that offenses have become spread out, more pass happy, and much more productive in recent times. Of the top 10 most prolific team total offense (rushing and passing) performances for a season in Carleton history, all of them happened after 1985. Of the top 10 career individual rushing leaders, all but one galloped to fame after 1979. All of the top 10 career passing leaders played after 1982. The young man who, if he stays healthy, will probably become Carleton's all-time passing leader, Jack Curtis, has one more season to play in 2025. If he does well, he will own all the passing records. It helps immensely that today's Knights sometimes toss the rock 55 or more times in a game. Offenses are rolling, and defenses are evolving to try to stop them. The strategic back-and-forth that makes football so very compelling has never changed, and Sully's book proves it.

Knights of the Gridiron represents an incredibly important contribution to the history of athletics at Carleton College. Other colleges and universities should be so lucky to possess such a treasure. The book is extremely well-written, meticulous in its research and detail, and highly entertaining to read. It is a really fun book.

Sully summarized how he thought about *Knights*: "Part of the point of view which should make this book something of value is the fact that football at a school of Carleton's type is totally at odds with the image it has as it compares with Division I, Division II and many other Division III programs. Where academics are so powerfully recognized and all-consuming, an A student in high school can be reduced to academic humility overnight. The football experiences at Carleton often become a safety net and provide rewarding respite from the academic rigors.

The team concept is truly real and of value at Carleton. Carleton football is a family in almost every sense. Most of our players keep in touch with each other for a lifetime.

This is a tribute to the hundreds of young men who played with passion for the Knights over the years. Carleton students are highly competitive by nature and our goal was always to be competitive but to have fun while playing football. I think we accomplished that. It has been a totally fulfilling and rewarding experience for me and my family and we all thank our 'other family' from the bottom of our hearts."

CHAPTER 18

Love & Loss

*"The sirens break the silence of the night
The raindrops on my window
Remind me that you're still here."*

BOB SULLIVAN

Shirley Sullivan lost her long battle with cancer at home in Northfield, on Oct. 14, 2010, surrounded by her family. Mass of Christian Burial took place a few days later at the Church of St. Dominic's. She was buried at the Calvary Cemetery in Northfield. Her loss was deeply felt by all those many people who knew and loved her, but most especially by her husband and children.

Her obituary read in part: "Shirley worked in various capacities throughout her life including secretarial work, clerking and managing Champion Sports in Northfield for 10 years. She enjoyed traveling, spending time at the lake cabin in Crosslake, having coffee with her many friends and mostly enjoying her children and grandchildren. Bob and Shirley celebrated their 50th wedding anniversary in 2007. Shirley was a vivacious, beautiful woman noted for her honesty, sincerity, compassion, pervasive sense of humor and unswerving loyalty and love for her husband and family."

I've read enough history to know this isn't how we do it, but in my opinion, at the end of the day, when judging a person's life, the first and most important testimony should come from the spouse and children, the ones who were closest to that person. What they say should matter more than any other consideration in examining the totality of a person's life and legacy.

Oldest daughter Stacy said of her mom, "She was beautiful and funny and the rock of our family. There was never a stranger to our door, everyone was welcome, especially dad's players. She would make them dinner; if a guy needed a bed for the night or a few days, he could stay with us.

She had a funny saying when the fall was upon us: 'We interrupt this marriage to bring you the football season.' We always said that the priorities for us were faith, family and football. But during the season, I was never sure of the order of those priorities. Mom went to all the games, every one. She would typically sit apart from the crowd; she didn't like to hear criticism if we lost. She was loving and fun but feisty and tough too. She was the occasionally fierce Mama Bear of the house."

Stacy continued: "I had a great dad. Football season was a challenge, but we always tried to eat dinner together, even if he came in late. The only time he really wasn't around was when he was out recruiting. I never felt that he was absent as a dad. He bought me new ice skates and took me to the pond and taught me to figure skate, even though he really didn't know how to skate himself. We did a lot of camping in the summer. He took us on trips to the southern part of the country, and we visited famous football stadiums. He loved history so we saw various historic sites. He took us out to the pizza parlor and to the movies.

We bought a cabin on Crosslake in 1990 and enjoyed spending time there. It was only a one-bedroom, but we all piled in. Eventually they added on a room, and Tim bought a cabin next door. We had great family times there. Growing up, we were all very close. The siblings are still close to this day.

My dad taught me that it's important to love what you do. He felt like he never worked a day in his life, because he loved football so much. He never cared about money or material things. I've tried to pass those values on to my own kids."

Oldest son Tim remembered his mom: "She was awesome, a great woman. She was fun, funny, loving, and tough. I recall her letting people have it in the stands at football games, if she didn't like something they said. She really supported my dad in his coaching career. All the kids loved coming over to our house, because of her. Everyone was welcome. She really liked to have fun. We went on trips, but never the expensive kind. Family road trips, camping. When we bought the cabin on Crosslake, that was a big deal. Lots of great family times there."

As for his dad: "My dad is my best friend forever. With all the big decisions in my life, I have sought his counsel, and his advice is always spot on. He taught me to stay calm in a crisis. He coached us in all our sports growing up. He even coached hockey, but he was in a pair of boots on the ice since he didn't know how to skate. Very funny. He pushed me to excel, but he was never hard on me. He'd say, you need to make 10 free throws in a row before we go in for dinner. Stuff like that.

He was a renaissance man. He loved to learn. He had a deep love of books and believed in the importance of education. Our faith was important too. We went to church every Sunday, without fail."

Bubba reminisced about Shirley: "My mom was really interesting because on the one hand she had this huge heart; she was really a caring lady. On the other hand, she was tough and competitive. She defended Carleton and her husband and her family like a Mama Bear. She would get mad and ground us for a week; then an hour later she would cool off and say, 'Okay, you're not grounded anymore.' She gave us lots of freedom but insisted that we make good decisions.

We went camping a lot. Dad loved camping, but mom hated it. Bugs and snakes were not her thing. But she went along and we always had fun. Mom worked at the sporting goods store in downtown Northfield. The guys would come in and if someone needed help with a purchase, she would try to make it happen for him. She was a very big-hearted person."

As for his dad, Bubba would echo much of what Tim said. We know how close the relationship between father and son became once Bubba turned his interest and talents to football.

The baby of the family, Molly, said this about her mom: "She was a super warm, loving and fun person. She loved dad's players. They were like big brothers to me; some of them literally lived with us from time to time. A funny thing about my mom is that as much as she cared for all of them, she had favorites among the players who she loved just like they were her own: Curt Wyffels, Jamie Jurkovich, Scott Wilhelmy, and the Nielson bros, among others. Whenever I saw any of those guys in later years, it always brought back happy memories of my mom. Also, a little-known fact about her: she was a lip kisser! If she liked you, when she greeted you, you would get kissed on the lips. I'd warn my friends, "Okay, she's a lip kisser.' We were a very close family. There were lots of hugs and kisses in our house."

About her dad: "He was great. We would go on fun trips. We never flew anywhere, we drove. Dad was a camper, mom hated camping. We would go on his baseball trips. He had us involved in sports year-round; he felt like it kept us busy and out of trouble. You didn't need to be the best performer, but he expected you to make your best effort, always. My dad is sort of a trip, that one. About 90 percent of the time, he is steady as a rock; what you see is what you get. But then there is the occasional wild hair, when he does something really funny and unexpected."

Sully's players adored Shirley too. She was like a second mom to so many of them.

Scott Wilhelmy recalled that he and his roommates arranged a kegger before the '79 season. Of course, Sully and Shirley were invited. Scooter said, "The Sullivans came early and knew when to leave too. But what I remember is that instead of clinging to Sully's side, Shirley was just everywhere, meeting all the players, asking about their hometowns and families and all of that. It was really amazing."

Scooter got to know her well. "You never needed an invitation to stop by the house. You were always welcome. She was outgoing, and she was the general in that house, but in a very nice way. She was opinionated but she was usually right. She was just a super lady. She really cared about people. And it was really fun to have a mom in town there in Northfield."

Ted Kluender said, "Shirley was just phenomenal, she was a great lady. She was kind of old school, but it was very clear that she cared about each and every one of us as not just a player, but as an important human being. She always had time for us; she was always present."

Jamie Jurkovich remembered: "Shirley was such a fan of Bob's and the program and the players. Met her early on, as a freshman, on the lawn outside of ground Burton. Must have been after the fall scrimmage or something. Had a picnic and a keg of beer, something like that. And Shirley is there socializing with all of us.

She was good to the Carleton players, and tried to give us deals at the sporting goods store on Division Street where she worked part-time. One of my teammates has a story about how she helped him out with cleats when he couldn't really afford them. I think she even put in a word to Sully for more playing time for me, because once it came up somehow and he rolled his eyes like, 'I know - she is on me about it.' A lot of players went to Shirley's funeral. Just the whole family made Carleton and Carleton football special."

What were Bob and Shirley like together? Molly said, "They were wonderful parents. Together, they instilled in us that you need to be a good person. When we got into trouble, it was because we were not being a good person. And we would be in even bigger trouble if we lied. Your word matters. They were both very accepting of others; my mom especially had a soft spot for the underdog. He really adored her. Sometimes she would get heated, and he would think it was funny and then she would get even madder. But they always made up.

Bubba remembered, "My parents were madly in love with each other. Growing up, for us kids, it was really a great relationship to witness. They did have their disagreements; but they would argue, and then it would be over. Everything was fine. That was a good thing to see. Their story together was an everlasting love story."

Tim said, "They were an extremely loving couple. My mom was headstrong and occasionally they would battle, but then it was over. They loved to have fun, they loved to dance. There was always loud country music playing in our house and they would dance. Together, they taught us kids how to love, how to say, 'I love you.'"

Stacy reminisced, "They would dance in the basement, to Johnny Cash, Johnny Horton, Waylon Jennings. I remember as a little girl standing on their feet and I would dance with them. We had fun together. We were a close family. They taught us to be close. I am still close to all my siblings today."

Shirley Dandurand was the love of Bob Sullivan's life. He knew the moment he laid eyes on her as a teenager that she would be his forever partner. They spent more than half a happy and eventful century together. They worked and played and danced and raised a wonderful family and impacted countless lives for the good, together. He cared for her, and she for him, throughout their life together, in sickness and in health.

He was so very sad, then, to have to say goodbye to her when the time finally came. One of the ways he eased his grief was to write poetry.

NIGHT AND DAY

"As the night bores into my soul
And the fears and fantasies erupt,
The dreams persist and become more real
With the ever increasing dark
Until the fear overcomes the reality

And reality becomes the fantasy.
Beauty and joy flee
As the demons continue to do battle
With my imagination.

As day makes its way into my world
The demons retreat and hope and life return.
Angels exist again
Love and joy become companions
And the sun once more warms my soul."

Sully's strong Catholic faith also helped him navigate the pain. "You are born into the faith," he said. "I grew up in the faith; went to Catholic grade school and a Catholic high school. I was probably an adolescent before I realized that not everyone in the world was Catholic. My first coaching job was at a Catholic school.

It's just been a huge part of my life. I don't agree with all the teachings of the Church. I hope the Church can continue to make progress. But it has helped me a lot during trying times, when things got hard. I believe in the power of prayer. My faith has been important in getting me through my days, through this life. I believe there is a reason for what happens; that the ultimate result is for the better. The ultimate result will have a positive effect for somebody. I was blessed with a wonderful wife and wonderful kids. I am blessed."

The sun once more warmed Sully's soul when, just over a year after Shirley passed away, he met a wonderful woman named Joanne Noyes. They were together and happy for 10 years when, sadly, Joanne slowly developed Alzheimer's and dementia. In recent years, she has been in assisted living. Ever the loyal and compassionate gentleman, Sully continues to visit her, despite her declining powers. She no longer knows who he is, but he knows his visits give her comfort.

In 2023, Sully met another terrific woman named Kathy Flanary. They are together and very much enjoying each other's company. Among other things, they love to dance.

I sat with Sully at his kitchen table, interviewing him for the book, on March 20, 2025, his 88th birthday. I brought him a goofy card and some Crown Royal (it's his favorite but he won't buy it because he thinks it's too expensive). During the time I spent with him, a little less than two hours, all four of his children called to wish him a happy birthday. If I am not mistaken, I believe they even called in their properly sequential birth order: Stacy first, then Tim, Bubba and then Molly.

After happy birthday wishes and pleasantries, all four calls ended with the tender exchange of these heartfelt words: "I love you."

CHAPTER 19

Sully & Me

"Our greatest glory is not in never falling, but in rising every time we fall."

CONFUCIUS

When my dear father died in July of 2022, I wrote an obituary in honor and commemoration of his long and eventful life. He was 95 years young when he finally went home. Sully read the piece in the *Star Tribune*, didn't know my dad had passed. He asked, "You wrote that, didn't you? I recognized your style. Your dad was an amazing guy." I replied, "Yes, I did, thanks. He was amazing. And I guess now that the old lion is dead, you are the closest I have to a father."

Sully said, "Okay."

Any one of the hundreds of guys who played ball for Coach Sullivan over the decades could write a chapter in his own book called, "Sully & Me." Here is my version.

My own sports journey was not dissimilar to Sully's. I grew up in the Minneapolis suburbs of Bloomington and Edina. Neither of my parents were interested in sports but, somehow, I got hooked. I started in baseball when I was 10 years old. Then football in the fall and basketball in the winter, just like Sully. Early on in grade school I realized that I could outrun all the other boys in a footrace. In junior high, I added track and field as a sport, just like Sully.

I played for a great football coach in Edina, Tom Moe, when I was 11 and 12. Tom had been a superb football and baseball athlete at Edina High School and then the University of Minnesota. He was also a top attorney in town, a managing partner at the Dorsey and Whitney law firm, and one of the people who influenced my decision to go to law school. He later became athletic director at the U. Over two seasons our teams were 15-1 and won two city championships. Tom was a terrific coach, and a really good man, but he was decidedly old school. We scrimmaged live and beat on each other at least once a week all throughout the season, for example.

Edina High School split into two schools, East and West, in 1972 (declining enrollment brought the schools back together eight years later.) I attended West and played football for the legendary Stavros Canakes. Local sportswriter Patrick Reusse once called Stav, "perhaps the most famous high school football coach in Minnesota history."

Stav coached at Edina from 1961 through 1989 and during that time won 203 games, 16 conference titles, and five state championships. He was a big, burly guy who had been a football star himself at the U of M, then played professionally in Canada. He was a Korean War Army veteran. He was old school and tough. Occasionally, he treated us harshly and we feared his wrath. But under his leadership, we played hard and straight ahead, brought the lumber, and won football games. We were 7-2 and co-champions of the Lake Conference Blue Division in my senior season.

In track at Edina West, I captained a team that won the Lake Conference title, then won our Region, and finished seventh among big schools in the state meet.

My point is that by the time I arrived at Carleton, I was used to old school coaching but also a hell of a lot of winning. A significant number of my teammates were, too. This made the football experience there all the more jarring.

When I arrived on campus in the fall of 1976, the program was in shambles. We suffered lopsided losses week after week. It did not get any better. In my sophomore year, playing for a coaching staff that I did not respect, I was suddenly benched for reasons that were never explained to me but that I could surmise. I reluctantly quit the team in disgust. It pained me to no end that I had let my teammates down, but I could no longer abide the blithe acceptance of pathetic and atrocious as our standard. Standing on the sideline, there was nothing I could do to help.

I wrote a letter to then-President Robert Edwards. In it I said, "The Carleton College football program is a disgrace and an embarrassment to what is otherwise recognized as an excellent institution... I think a school like Carleton should strive for excellence in all fields, not just academics. An opportunity to achieve a fine, well-rounded experience is one of the goals a student should be able to seek in college."

I am not taking any credit for what transpired next; there were more powerful voices than mine, including members of the Board of Trustees, who felt the same way. We were all tired of losing. There was one more disastrous season and then change happened. A new sheriff rode into town, and his name was Bob Sullivan.

I first met Sully at some forgotten banquet in the winter of 1979, near the end of my junior year. He proceeded to aggressively re-recruit me to come back out for football. He sent me a note in campus mail (I still have it) telling me he needed speed such as mine to run his wide-open style of offense. During the winter season he came down to the indoor track at Laird Stadium and watched me run the 60-yard dash. He courted and cajoled and finally convinced me. In short, he made me feel, just as he did every single one of his other players, like an important individual. I enthusiastically came back out to play ball for him, for one last hurrah. My life was changed forever.

Of the many lessons that I learned from Sully, during that single season and in the decades beyond as we have stayed in close touch, two stand out. First, the idea that human beings respond and perform better when they are treated respectfully, rather than punitively, really resonated with me. Second, I learned and witnessed the critical importance of perseverance in all things. Don't give up when life gets hard; keep fighting until you succeed.

I decided in my sophomore year at Carleton to volunteer to become a

Marine infantry officer upon graduation. I wanted to serve our country, and I thirsted for an adventure. Both wishes were granted. I spent two summers – 12 weeks total - in Officer Candidate School. When football started in August 1979, I had just returned from "boot camp" in Quantico, Virginia. I was commissioned a second lieutenant when I graduated and served for three years from August of 1980.

What a fantastic leadership experience it was, and a great opportunity to apply recent lessons learned. I started out as a rifle platoon leader, with 42 Marines under my command. My initial immature and unthinking approach was to be the typical hard-ass Marine officer. But I soon realized that just wasn't me; it didn't feel right. I was not an old school kind of guy.

I took a chapter from the Book of Sully, calmed down, grew up, started treating the young men in my charge like men, making sure they knew I cared about each of them (which I did), and enjoyed much greater success.

By the time I got out as a first lieutenant, I was in a captain's billet as a rifle company commander, with literally life-and-death responsibility for 150 Marines. Oh, and the perseverance piece was important too. It was a very challenging time in my life. There were some hard days. But I'll never forget it because I learned and grew so much.

I attended graduate school at the University of Wisconsin-Madison, where I earned a combined juris doctor and master's degree in public policy and administration. I practiced law as a litigator for a few years in the Twin Cities in the late '80s, then embarked on a long business career.

My wife Faith and I met in Madison and have been married for 40 years. We have two adult daughters, Anna and Lucia, who are off on their own and good, productive citizens. We are a close, loving family. When the girls were growing up, I told them our family motto is, "Never give up." They used to laugh at me when I repeated that over and over. But then they got older and faced life's trials and tribulations and realized that it was really good advice. They have both courageously overcome numerous obstacles over the years.

I fought the corporate wars for a combined 16 years, working in various leadership roles, first for Target Corporation and then the Best Buy Company. While at Best Buy, in 2007, I tapped into my deep love of history and knowledge of the corporate world to develop an experiential leadership program based on visits to Gettysburg, Pennsylvania (site of the famous 1863 battle in the American Civil War) and Little Bighorn, Montana (site of Custer's Last Stand in 1876). Best Buy was highly supportive of this effort. I later added programs based on the incredible western journey of Lewis and Clark from 1804 to 1806, and the epic Apollo space missions of the 1960s.

In 2009, at the onset of the Great Recession, Best Buy offered a buyout to all its corporate employees. I took a generous severance and formed my own company, now called Blue Knight Leadership, LLC. I weathered tough economic times, and have been doing leadership and business consulting, as well as taking corporate teams to historic venues, ever since. I enjoy being my own boss. They say that if you're going to work for an idiot, it might as well be yourself.

Over the almost 20 years of running my program, more than 1,000 leaders at every level from many organizations in all kinds of industries have trained with me. In what I teach about the timeless lessons of leadership, among many other things, the importance of strong relationships, ironclad trust, honest communication, and dogged perseverance have always been front and center. What I learned from Coach Sullivan has profoundly impacted both my personal and professional lives.

Okay, now let's have some fun telling Sully stories. Every guy who played for him has his favorites. Here are some of mine.

Over the years since we graduated, my teammates have always chuckled and had a running joke that sort of stumped me. They claimed that Sully had a habit, when he was on a roll and forcefully articulating his points one at a time, of saying, "First of all, A) blah blah, 2) yada yada, and C) blah blah." A), 2) and C)?! No way would he do that. The least of the problems with that is that it's not properly sequential. If I had ever heard him say that I didn't remember it. They swore to it. "Listen to him sometime," they recommended. So I did, standing with him in his kitchen a number of years ago. He was on a rant about something, maybe politics, maybe how much he hates the Oles,

I don't remember. And he said, "Now listen Jeff, first of all A), and 2), and C) blah blah."

I smiled to myself, "Shit, the boys were right. He really does do that. And it's really, really funny."

Scott Wilhelmy, my classmate and teammate, was an excellent football player and one of the best baseball players in Carleton history. He was a left-handed hitting catcher, who struck out maybe four or five times in his entire career. With Sully's help, pro scouts took a look at Scooter and he was drafted by the Minnesota Twins in the late rounds in 1980. He played a year of professional ball with the Twins' Class A affiliate in Visalia, California, then came back to Carleton to coach with Sully.

For whatever reason, try though we might, we could never get Scoots into the C-Club Hall of Fame. He must have pissed someone off along the way. Finally, again with Sully's help, we got him into the Hall 40 years after the fact, in 2020. Our time in the wilderness was over.

There was a pandemic and so the induction ceremony was going to be via Zoom. Scooter and I would participate on the call with Sully in his home. I drove down from the 'burbs at the appointed hour, only to find major construction near Sully's place. Somehow, I got onto the wrong side of Northfield High School and could not navigate via GPS to get to his home. Scooter had arrived at Sully's via some mysterious route. He sent Sully to walk out to the front of the school, a few blocks away, to meet and ride home with me. The ceremony would begin soon.

Sully did not have his phone. I could not contact him. And I could not get to him. Finally, I asked some fine citizen who was walking his dog how to get there, and he directed me around the construction. I was quite tardy when I finally pulled up to Coach. He had his arms crossed and was tapping his foot. He got into the car.

"Where the hell were ya?!"

"Coach, I was trying to get to you but there's all this construction."

"Well, first of all, A) I been standing here for about 15 minutes! 2) I live right over there! And C) You have no excuse, 'cause you've been there before!"

"Coach, I know where you live. I just couldn't get there from where I was."

Scooter called. "Apple, you got the Coach?"

"Yeah, I got him, we're on our way."

"Okay, ask him what's his internet password. I want to get on my laptop and we're about to start."

"Oh boy, let's see how this goes," I thought to myself.

"Coach, Scooter wants to know what's your internet password?"

"How the hell should I know?!"

"It's your friggin' internet connection, in your house."

"I don't know it." (He later remembered that the password was "Shirley.")

We finally arrived just in time and watched the ceremony on Sully's own desktop, which was internet connected, sitting together on the bed in his bedroom. Yes, I know, weird visual.

Later, I said to him, "When we were in the car, I thought, I'm 62 years old and I'm getting yelled at by my 82-year-old football coach, again."

"I was not yelling. And I never yelled at you guys."

He was right. He never really did yell at us. He made his point emphatically from time to time, but he never yelled.

In 2022, a group of football alums came up with the idea of naming the football field at Laird Stadium after our beloved Bob Sullivan. We approached the development office at Carleton and were told that it was very doable, if we could raise one million dollars for naming rights. We proceeded to do just that, and the Sullivan Fund (the Fund) was established.

The dedication ceremony took place on October 15, 2022, at halftime of that afternoon's homecoming game. Three hundred of Sully's loyal former players showed up from all over the country to pay their respects and celebrate with their Coach. There was a banquet that evening. When asked later what it felt like to be honored in that way Sully said, "Overwhelming."

In August of 2023, the College entered into an agreement with an entity called Carleton Football Excellence (CFE). This Minnesota nonprofit was formed to represent the interests of the football alumni who were the donors to the Fund. I was the first president of CFE but resigned recently to focus on the writing of this book. Steve Huffer is now our very capable president.

The purpose of the fund is to pay for football-only expenses and to be budget additive to the annual football budget. Coach Tom Journell has used the interest that the Fund kicks off to pay for things that would not normally be covered in his regular budget. Sully was of course highly supportive of the effort and is happy that a Fund named for him will continue to benefit the football program in perpetuity.

I signed the contract with the College for CFE in August of '23. I proceeded to meet with Coach Journell first and then, later that same day, Sully, to walk each of them through the terms of the contract.

Sully had a particular interest in one of the sections of the document, known as the "moral turpitude" clause. This language is standard in a naming agreement of this type. It reads, "There could arise in the future unforeseen extraordinary circumstances where the College determines that naming the Fund or Field for Bob Sullivan compromises the public trust and or reputation of the College, due, for example, to credible claims of moral turpitude by Bob Sullivan..."

I could tell he was listening very carefully as I explained this to him. He asked me to repeat the contract language. He really didn't listen to much of anything I told him after that. As I was leaving, he walked me out to my car.

"So, Jeff, you're a lawyer, just what would I have to do to trigger that moral turpitude thing?"

"I don't know Coach, you know, stuff like bad behavior on the internet."

"Yeah? What else."

"I don't know Coach [it was getting a bit awkward discussing moral turpitude with my old ball coach], stuff like messing around with underage women."

"How young?" he inquired.

"I don't know Coach. You know, younger than 18. Like 17 and below. Underage."

"W'hell, when I think about underage women these days, I'm going for 65 and below. Will that be a problem?" He had a smile on his face.

"Ah, no Coach, I believe we would be okay under the turpitude clause if we stay in that age range. You're good."

Speaking of women, and Sully adores women, he always loved the wives of his former players. He thought that every single one of us was not nearly good enough for the women we married. He beleived those gals were all smarter, better-looking, and more talented than anything any one of his boys deserved.

"W'hell, how any of you guys scored a wife like that is beyond me. You guys all way outkicked your coverage. Way. Outkicked. Coverage. Every one of you."

I learned way more about football from Sully sitting on his couch watching it on TV with him than I ever did when he was my coach. He taught me to see the game in a much more holistic way. There is a great quote from the excellent book, *Take Your Eye Off the Ball 2.0*, by Pat Kirwan. These could have been the exact words that Sully would speak on this topic: "In order to watch football from a new vantage point, I'm asking you to break the cardinal rule that every coach teaches every kid the first time he or she takes the field, whether it's a gridiron or a diamond, a basketball court or a tennis court. I want you to take your eye off the ball.

I want you to see the offensive linemen executing blocking assignments that are as intricate as they are intense. I want you to notice the safety sneaking up into the box before the snap, confusing a quarterback who's trying to figure out where the pressure will be coming from. I want you to notice which players are in the game and anticipate what's about to happen. When you take your eye off the ball, you'll be amazed at how much action, athleticism, and gamesmanship you've been missing." All good advice with which Sully would strongly concur.

Sully was never a tough guy kind of coach, but he recognized that the application of physical force to achieve an objective was a huge part of the game. The team that chops wood harder would most often prevail. That's why Sully loved his linebackers.

He said to me one afternoon, "I loved my linebackers. Why, this guy was All-Conference in both the MWC and the MIAC. This guy was an All-America. This guy was our all-time leading tackler. This guy led the conference in tackles…" He went on and on. (If you want to know who he was talking about, go to the linebacker section of the next chapter.) He finally ran out of gas and looked at me, maybe sensed that I was jealous or thought he was overdoing it on the linebacker love theme (I wasn't, and I didn't). He said, "W'hell, you know, we needed guys like you too. You know, 'pretty boy' wide receivers. You know, the kind of guy who looks in the locker room mirror BEFORE the game and combs his hair." Got it, Coach, thanks.

I once asked Sully who he thought was the greatest NFL head coach ever, Vince Lombardi or Bill Belichick. He said, "Neither. It's Bill Walsh." I said, "That's interesting. You may be right. You know the problem with Bill Belichick is that he was tragically born without a personality."

Sully said, "What did you just say?" He started to laugh.

"I said Belichick was tragically born without a personality." (I think this was a movie line I had heard years ago.)

"Hold on," he said. "I gotta get a piece of paper and a pencil and write that down." I repeated the line for a third time. He scribbled it for his files. He continued to chuckle for the rest of the afternoon.

Just recently, Bill Belichick published a book called, *The Art of Winning* (I read it, quickly; it's an okay book; B or B-minus on the grading scale kind of stuff; BTW, did you know Belichick – age 73 - has a 24-year-old girlfriend? He should write a book about how he pulled that off.)

I called Sully and said, "Hey Coach, did you see that Belichick wrote a book? It's called, *Tragically Born Without a Personality: My Life Story*, by Bill Belichick. We laughed some more.

One time, when Sully was about 85 and I was about 65, he looked at me and said, somewhat hesitantly, "Here's the thing, Jeff. I think I'm still a really cool guy."

I emphatically reassured him: "You are Sully. You are still a really, really cool guy."

CHAPTER 20

THE PANTHEON

Sully's All-Time Knights Team, 1979-2000

"A good coach will make his players see what they can be rather than what they are."

ARA PARSEGHIAN

C oach Sullivan spent considerable time pondering the question of which three football players at each position or position group were the very best among all the athletes he coached from 1979 through his final 2000 season. Sully keenly recognizes that many great players preceded his era, and many great ones have come since. These are the truly elite of some 500 or so Knights that he coached over 22 years.

Carleton football records are current as of 2025. The Matt Zell Award is presented annually to the sophomore player who demonstrates the most dedication and loyalty to the football program; the C.J. Hunt Award goes to the player who shows the most improvement; the Lippert Memorial Award honors the player who contributes the most to the football team. Carleton moved from the Midwest Conference to the MIAC and began naming a team MVP in 1983. The Carleton C-Club came into being in 1976. Nineteen former coaches and athletes were inducted into the inaugural Hall of Fame class. As of 2025, there are more than 200 individual members of the Hall of Fame; three teams have also been inducted, including the 1954 undefeated Midwest Conference championship football team.

The following is a brief description of each player's career highlights. Sully then provides his recollections and commentary, in quotes, about each player, from a series of interviews in late 2024.

Understand that these are the musings of an 87-year-old man who was, in some cases, looking as far as 45 years into the past. While his mental acuity and recall of detail are utterly astonishing, his memory is undoubtedly imperfect. For those who are intensely interested in the content of this chapter, please be patient and kind, lest we come around when you are 87 to see how much you remember ("What did I have for breakfast this morning? Do I have socks on? Hmmm...")

With that said, Game On: Let the angst, weeping, gnashing of teeth, and heated barroom debates begin!

DEFENSIVE LINEMEN/TACKLES:

Mike Stam (1985-'87) was a local kid from Faribault, Minnesota. He was big, strong and fast, with the ability and potential to play professional football. An All-MIAC second-team selection as a sophomore, he dominated the league in his junior season to earn first-team honors. His 17 career sacks had him on track to become Carleton's all-time leader. Mike died tragically in a snowmobile accident in January 1988, a great athlete and even better human being whose exemplary life was cut short. In his honor the MIAC, working with Coach Sullivan and the Stam family, established the Mike Stam Award in 1990, which is presented each season to the league's outstanding lineman.

"First of all, Mike was a great person and a great leader in terms of, I would say, protecting anybody in sight that needed physical protection. He was astounding. He was fast, strong, aggressive, quick, you name it. He was a pro prospect, for sure. I've told the story 100 times about Murray Warmath, who was an NFL scout for the Vi-

kings. Murray scouted Mike hard and predicted that he would have gone by the fourth round of the NFL draft, had he lived. Mike would have led our team in career tackles for an interior lineman had he played that senior year. He would have led in career sacks, all of it, without a doubt."

Scott Bunnell (1986-'89) was a highly touted high school recruit out of Palo Alto, California. He could have gone Division I but chose Carleton instead, earning first-team All-MIAC honors in 1988 and 1989. He had 19.5 career sacks to rank sixth in school history. In 1989, he became the first Knight defensive lineman to earn All-American status. He was truly a sentimental favorite when he won the prestigious Mike Stam Award in 1989 as the MIAC's premier lineman. Scott was inducted into the Carleton C-Club Athletic Hall of Fame in 2010.

"Those two guys [Stam and Bunnell] were line mates. Scott was also a very talented defensive lineman. He was the second winner of the Mike Stam Award. He was an All-American defensive tackle who was out of the San Francisco area. He was a Division I prospect for sure in both football and track. He was looked at by the pro scouts also. He was a dominant player, period. He was big and fast, smart, all of it. He belonged in Division I, but he didn't want any part of major college football and came to Carleton instead. He just wanted to live his life and not be a big name like he was out on the West Coast when he was in high school. I guess he just wanted to get away from some of that hoopla out there and he came to Carleton and excelled. He was a religion major, by the way, of all things."

Pat Rowan (1993-'96) was a dominant defensive lineman who won All-MIAC honors in 1995. Pat was sixth all-time in 1995 with 16 tackles for loss in the season, totaling 61 yards. In that same season, he also registered 53 total tackles, seven sacks, and two fumble recoveries.

"Pat was a graduate of Hill Murray, my former school. He was a big, really aggressive, quick kid. He got hurt his senior year, I think, and didn't play a lot that year. But he was very talented. He was with a group of three other guys that were in his era that were also good. And we had a really good defensive line. In fact, that was the best defensive line we had over the years, other than the Stam/Bunnell line. Pat finished his career All-Conference, all that good stuff."

DEFENSIVE LINEMEN/ENDS:

Troy Ethen (1984-'87) was a four-year starter on the defensive line. He is fourth on the Knights' career list with 22 sacks. In 1985 he received the Zell Award and was All-Conference Honorable Mention. He was an All-MIAC second team pick the following season, and as a senior captain in 1987 he recorded 4.5 sacks in a single game against Augsburg. He also set the program record with 10 sacks that season and made the All-MIAC first team. Troy is in the C-Club Hall of Fame.

"Troy was a Division I or II prospect out of Austin, Minnesota. His school was called Austin Pacelli High School in those days. I think he hesitated in coming to Carleton, but he came from a very large family, and we were able to help him with some financial aid. Based on that I worked very hard to talk him into coming. He hadn't thought much about it till I got to him. He turned down several Division II offers to come to Carleton and academically, like a lot of my guys, he was very well qualified with a 4.0 in high school. He was very good defensively as an end. He was one of the all-time sack leaders during my era. One of the leaders in career tackles. He was big, strong, fast. He had all the athletic attributes you'd want in a defensive end."

J.J. Franz (1997-'00) was a ferocious defensive end who is tied as Carleton's all-time sack leader with 25.5 (Jeff Thurk also has 25.5.) J.J. was All-MIAC first team and a team captain in 1999 and 2000. He was also honored as an Honorable Mention All-America in his senior year.

"J.J. Franz was a local kid from Northfield, Minnesota. He's a cousin to Tim Franz, one of my first captains back in '79. He was an inside linebacker in high school, played for my son Bubba, led them in tackles, was all everything in high school. He came to Carleton, and I think he enjoyed himself here. I moved him to defensive end from inside linebacker with the new defense we put in when he got here. He was relatively small but extremely quick and very, very aggressive. He was the all-time leader in career sacks and among the leaders in sacks in a season, all that sort of thing. He put up some great numbers, but his key attributes were his desire and his quickness. He just loved contact and wasn't afraid of anybody. He was a football player, for sure."

Jeff Thurk (1997-'00) and J.J. Franz were a terrific tandem at defensive end and played all four years together. They are co-leaders in all-time sacks with 25.5 apiece. Jeff hailed from Eden Prairie, Minnesota, where he played on the first of the great Mike Grant's (son of the great Bud Grant) 11 state championship teams in 1996. Jeff was versatile and could have played any position across the defensive front. He is tied for first at Carleton with 10 sacks in a season in both 1999 and 2000. Jeff was a team captain in his senior season.

"Jeff was just a very talented defensive end who could do anything we wanted him to do here, play inside or outside, and what we call the seven or nine techniques. Either one of them. He could also play the ten technique in space too [a defensive lineman in seven technique lines up on the inside shoulder of the tight end, and positions himself even further outside the offensive end man in the nine and ten techniques.] So Jeff was very versatile. And his statistics around sacks speak for themselves. He and J.J. were both just excellent."

DEFENSIVE LINEMEN/NOSEGUARDS

(Sully's defenses featured a noseguard until 1992, when the Knights switched to the Bear Defense and changed from five to four defensive linemen; see Chapter 13 for a detailed description of the Bear Defense):

Andy Engel (1978-'81) was an absolute rock at noseguard, the best who ever played for Sully. Andy was stout and tough, but he moved well. He was extremely disruptive in the center of the defensive line and consistently drew double teams, enabling his brothers at linebacker to make tackles. Andy won the C.J. Hunt in 1980 and the Lippert in '81. He was All-Midwest Conference first team in 1981.

"Andy was there when I got there in 1979 and was an established starter at noseguard. He was big, active, and he was the kind of guy that you had to double team, which would free up linebackers to make tackles, which of course they're supposed to do. The famous quote is, apparently, I said it in film sessions more than once, 'Thank God for Andy Engel,' because he was making plays that most guys don't make. He was out of St. Thomas Academy, by the way. He was just solid, and a great individual kid too."

Dave Gunnarson (1987-'90) was also a force at noseguard but was fully capable of playing all five spots on the defensive front. He was taller than the typical noseguard and, like Andy Engel, he moved well and was extremely disruptive to offensive schemes. Dave received the Lippert Trophy in 1990.

"At different points in this career, Dave did play elsewhere on the defensive line, at tackle and end, but he started out as a noseguard. He was tall, about 6 foot 3. He was disruptive, agile, and had very good feet. He was also very smart with a good football I.Q. Since his playing days he has been very active and loyal to Carleton football."

Billy Ray Peterson (1983-'86) was an extremely solid noseguard, whose key attribute was his quickness. He is renowned for his legendary performance in the "Upset of the Decade," when Carleton defeated St. Thomas – who was ranked number one in the NCAA Region and number five in the nation at the time - on October 25, 1986. Billy Ray was named the MIAC defensive player of the week for his 11 tackles and three sacks on that day.

"Billy Ray was out of Blaine, which was a great pipeline for us, by the way. Davy Nelson [a legendary Minnesota coach who won state titles both at Blaine and, later, at Minnetonka High School] was a good friend of mine and the head coach at the time. He sent a bunch of players our way. For us, Billy had a lot of stats, sacks and stuff like that. Was player of the week for the 'Miracle Game.' Quick would be my first word with him. He smelled the football; he knew where the ball was, and he went and got there. Noseguards in general in that defense are not productive numerically. They are essential to the defense, especially when people have to double team them. If they don't double team him, and he's good, he is very disruptive, and Billy Ray was one of those for sure."

LINEBACKERS/INSIDE AND OUTSIDE

(Because Sully's defensive scheme frequently required his linebackers to play both inside and outside, he has named his six best all-around linebackers):

Todd Kuss (1981-'84) was a tackling machine who was All-Midwest Conference in 1982 and All-MIAC in 1983 (one of a small number of Sully's guys to be All-Conference in both leagues). But for lack of tackling statistics in the Midwest, Todd likely would have been Carleton's all-time leader. He was team MVP in 1983, won the Lippert and was team captain in 1984. Todd made 135 tackles in 1983, which was third all-time in a single season.

"Todd was a high school All-American out of Columbia Heights; he had several Division II offers, but he was too small for Division I. He was only 6 feet tall and maybe 205. But he was a great tackler, he just hit people. We did not keep stats in his first two years, but he led the team in tackles both years, as well as in his junior and senior years too. He would have been the school's all-time leader for sure had we kept track of those tackles. The other thing about him which was amazing is that he had eight career interceptions. For an inside linebacker that is unheard of. He also was team captain and won just about every other award we had along the way. He was All-Conference in both the Midwest and the MIAC. Hopefully he's in our C-Club Hall of Fame as of this year - he should have been in a long time ago [Todd Kuss was indeed finally inducted into the Hall of Fame in early 2025; Sully called him with the happy news, to Todd's great delight.] Yeah, one of the best ever. Well, actually, he was the best ever."

Scott O'Reilly (1998-'01) finished second in program history by the end of his career with 346 tackles. He made 143 tackles in 2001, the most ever in a season. He won the C.J. Hunt Award in 2000, as well as All-MIAC second-team honors. As a senior co-captain in 2001, he was named All-MIAC first-team and Honorable Mention All-America. Scott is a C-Club Hall of Famer who was inducted in 2017.

"Scott was from Rochester, Minnesota. He was an interesting cat. He was just a player. He just reacted. Gerald Young talked at Scott's Hall of Fame Induction. He spoke about the fact that Scott didn't really read keys, he just went to the ball and made the play. He made a hell of a lot of tackles in his career. Second leading tackler, I think, of all time. Scott was just a natural inside linebacker, a natural tackler, a natural pursuer of the football. Again, like most of my guys, he had a high IQ both on and off the field."

John Haberman (1986-'88) was an incredibly tough, versatile linebacker who transferred into Carleton to play for three seasons. In his senior year, he was All-MIAC and a team captain. John recorded a terrifically productive 125 tackles in 1986, for eighth all-time. He is third in career tackles with 338.

"John was a fun guy to be around. He was another transfer. He had gone on a full ride to I want to say Augustana, I think, and didn't like it. I recruited him in high school, and he went for the scholarship. He became dissatisfied and so transferred to Carleton and became a great, great linebacker. Don't have his stats in front of me, but he's in the top five or six tackling and sacks and all that good stuff. He could do it all. He had what they call a dual personality: off the field, very quiet, mild mannered. Yeah. Nice guy. But I always referred to him as one of those guys that when he got on the football field, he was foaming at the mouth. He was a mean son of a gun once he put the pads on, that's for sure."

John Heyneman (1985-'88) and John Haberman were teammates and together they struck fear into the hearts of opposing ball carriers. Heyneman was an all-around high school star who also played running back for the Knights but was finally moved to linebacker. In 1986 he made 142 tackles, which was good for second all-time in a season. He was All-MIAC in 1987. He is sixth on the career list with 310 tackles.

"John was a versatile linebacker. He was a good running back as well, who came out of a nine-man program in Montana where he was All-State. He played some running back for us, but he ended up making it at inside backer. He could cover pass receivers better than any linebacker we ever had in that respect. Great range because he was such a good overall athlete. I think if I'm not mistaken, he was a bronco rider in rodeos also. Again, a very western Montana guy, if ever there was one. Yeah, just a great all-around athlete who fit perfectly in our scheme."

Paul Moore (1982-'85) was a fierce and extremely decorated linebacker. He is one of the small number of athletes who won all three football trophies: the Zell Award in 1983; C.J. Hunt in 1984; and the Lippert Trophy in '85. Paul was All-MIAC and a team captain in 1985. He registered 292 career tackles, good for ninth on the all-time list.

"Paul was out of Worthington, Minnesota. He was one of our better leaders and developed nicely as time went on over two or three years. He was a very, very studious guy. Very football wise and into studying film. He analyzed film and that would help him call our defensive alignments as an inside backer. He led the team in tackles, was All-Conference and a team captain, of course. But I guess the word studious keeps

coming into my mind on him. He was a very Intellectual linebacker, if there's ever been such a thing" [said by Coach with a chuckle].

Matt Hoffman (1993-'96) was a terrific linebacker who won the Zell Trophy in 1994, and C.J. Hunt in 1995, when he was also a team captain. Matt made 280 career tackles, which puts him in the top 15 in school history.

"Matt Hoffman was also an interesting recruit. He was headed to Bethel. He was a very religious kid. But I convinced him to come to Carleton; I said, 'If you go to Bethel, everybody there is going to be like you, they're going to be religious, blah, blah blah. Just think if you come to Carleton, you could meet all kinds of people'; and so he came. He ended up being one of our greatest linebackers of all time. Leading tackler, captain of course. He just did a terrific job, and he was a real jewel at inside backer."

DEFENSIVE BACKS/CORNERS:

Tim Thull (1987-'90) was a tremendous two-sport athlete in football and baseball. He was twice named All-MIAC in each sport. In football, he was a ball-hawking cornerback and safety who, in 1990, led the conference in interceptions, helping him to gain recognition as an Honorable Mention All-American. Tim made 19 career interceptions, second all-time, and he was inducted into the C-Club Hall of Fame in 2011.

"Well, Tim is the best defensive back we ever had for sure. Again, a great athlete; two-sport athlete, baseball being his other sport. He could run, he could cover, he could have played anywhere in the secondary, and offensively he could have been a wideout or running back. Anything you want, just a great all-around athlete. Led the team in punt returns and interceptions. His interception total is second all-time. Tim started for four years, started the minute he walked on campus. He could do it all."

Josh Schroeder (1997-'00) was also an outstanding two-sport athlete. He won the Zell in 1998. In his senior season, he was a third-team All-America, All-MIAC, Lippert winner, team MVP, and team captain. Josh had 14 career interceptions, tied for third all-time. He entered the C-Club Hall of Fame in 2021.

"Josh was one of my last recruits. He was also one of my two last players [the other being J.J. Franz], in the year 2000, who made All-America. Josh was another great two-sport athlete; baseball was his other sport. Starter immediately, he could run, had good speed, good vision. Led the team every year in interceptions and ran a couple of them back for touchdowns, if I'm not mistaken. Our best defensive back my last four years of my career, and everything you can say about the attributes of the best defensive backs, he had those skills."

Karl Thomas (1979-'82) was a smart and hard-nosed cornerback, who was a four-year starter. He was All-MIAC and a team captain in his senior season. Karl made 11 career interceptions, which puts him in the top 10 all-time.

"Karl was part of my first very first recruiting class, and he and John Sieben were buddies. They were the starting corners pretty much for all four years they were here. They were both excellent. Karl was especially smart, and he could run. He was out of St. Cloud, Minnesota. We got him away from St. John's, by the way. He was very steady, a leader, team captain. His stats speak for themselves, interception-wise and tackles and all that good stuff. He did everything we could ask of any defensive back and especially our corners. He could cover, I mean, he could really cover guys, man-to-man and so on, whatever we needed him to play."

DEFENSIVE BACKS/SAFETIES:

Art Gilliland (1989-'92) was an outstanding safety and one of the key players who led Carleton to the MIAC title in 1992, earning All-MIAC and All-America honors that year. His 129 tackles in 1992 ranks sixth on Carleton's single season list. He made 312 career tackles, fifth all-time. He was named the team's Zell Award winner in 1990 and took home the Lippert in 1992. Art was also an outstanding wrestler who qualified for the NCAA Championships in 1990. He made the C-Club Hall of Fame in 2003.

"Well, Art was a great, great safety. He was an absolute natural for safety when we installed our new defense in '92 [the Bear Defense is a high-risk scheme because it puts many defenders close to the line of scrimmage and leaves just one high free safety.] He was a lone wolf. The corners were man-to-man. He was the only safety we had, and he had to cover everything and support the run as well. He was so gifted athletically,

that he could do that. He was from out West, California, I think. He was the key cog in that defense, that Bear defense we played. Without him being there and being as good as he was, we would not have been as successful or won the MIAC. He made All-American, of course, and legitimately so. He was very deserving of that honor."

Al Stier (1992-'95) was a tremendously versatile football player and one of the best multi-sport athletes in Carleton history. In 1994 he secured five interceptions, tied for ninth all-time in a season. He won the Lippert Award and was a team captain in 1995.

"Al was a great all-around athlete and could have played anywhere. He played some offense; he could pass, could have been a heck of a quarterback, for that matter. We ran the official Motown play [a long lateral pass to a receiver who then in turn passes deep downfield] with him. I can't tell you how many times he lined up at wide receiver and threw the double pass. He was also sometimes on the receiving end of the double pass. Most of his career was spent at free safety. He had a great interception total. Team captain. He lettered in five sports at Carleton, if you can imagine that. Football, basketball, baseball, track, golf, I think. Anyway, of all the sports he lettered in he played just a year or two in each one of them, of course, except for football. But yeah, he was something else."

Dave Adams (1984-'87) was one of Carleton's all-time greats at safety. He had 11 interceptions in 1985, which is tied for most ever in a season. During that season he returned a punt 98 yards against Hamline. He earned All-MIAC honors in 1987. Dave's 25 career interceptions put him first all-time.

"Dave was always in the mix. He was a pure free safety. He was not a tackler necessarily, but he was a defender and a leader. He's got the career interception record. He was a great ball hawk. Against Hamline one year they completed a pass down the middle. He grabbed it out of the receiver's hands and ran it back 70 yards for a touchdown. He made interceptions all over. He was a 6-foot-4 basketball player also, and just a natural athlete. He was like Paul Krause of the Vikings back in the day [Krause is the all-time interception leader in NFL history.] And again, Dave was just a real good ball hawk back there."

OFFENSIVE LINEMEN/TACKLES:

Guy Finne (1985-'88) was a talented all-around athlete who was a superb offensive tackle and one of Carleton's best ever. He was an incredibly hard worker who was big, strong, and moved extremely well. Guy was named first-team All-MIAC and All-America Honorable Mention in 1988.

"Guy was from a small town here in Minnesota, and he was a great high school athlete, and a great basketball player too. He was the best offensive tackle that I have ever coached. Very agile, great feet, smart. He worked at his game. He was the type of guy that loved football. I used to come to the stadium early on game day Saturday mornings when we were at home. He would be out on the field walking around all by himself at like 9:00 in the morning. I guess he was getting ready for the game in his own way. He was also looked at by the Green Bay Packers. Interesting story. They wanted to fly him in during the spring to look at him and I went to his dorm. I said 'Guy, Green Bay wants you to fly you in for a tryout.' And he said, 'I can't go.' I said, 'What do you mean you can't go?' He said, 'I hate to fly' and so he didn't go; but he could have gone and could have had a tryout. Who knows if he might have made it? He was a big kid, extremely agile. He could do whatever he wanted on the offensive line, for sure."

Steve Huffer (1979-'80) was an extremely talented tackle who only played for two years but was dominant throughout his brief career. Steve was All-Mid-west Conference in 1979 and 1980, and won the Lippert Award and an All-America Honorable Mention in 1980. He was also All-Conference as a weight man in track and field.

"Steve was there when I arrived in '79. He was a transfer from West Point and also Franklin College in Indiana. He was from Indianapolis and played for us for two years, in '79 and '80. All-Conference, of course, both years. He was big and smart as hell and just dominated whoever he was playing against. It became almost comical. The best story about him is with Brian Davies. Davies was the tight end, and the play called for a double team down on the defensive tackle, with Huffer and Davies. They were getting into their stance and Huffer looks at Davies and says, 'Don't bother. I got this guy. Go find a linebacker.' Davies says, 'Okay' and that was that. That's kind of the way things were with Huffer. He was that good and just very experienced. By the

time I got there, I didn't have to coach him at all, I just had to plug him in and let him play. But yeah, he was obviously outstanding."

Paul Johnson (1980-'83) was a force at offensive tackle who was sufficiently talented to generate interest from NFL scouts. He dominated opponents at the line of scrimmage. Paul earned first-team All-Midwest Conference honors in 1981 and '82 and was an All-MIAC first teamer in 1983.

"Paul was another interesting dude out of Saint Louis Park, Minnesota. He did not like to train in the off-season, but in August he started getting ready to play football. He was All-Conference for three straight years in both the Midwest and the MIAC. Big kid, very talented. Great skills, good feet, dominant person. He could always take over the offensive line for us. He played well in every game, but the offseason was not his bag. But he got ready to play, every game and every season, no question about that. He's a doctor now, a very successful orthopedic surgeon. And so yeah, he was one of the three best-ever tackles. [Coach Sullivan was reminded of the great Jim Marshall, who was an outstanding defensive lineman for the Minnesota Vikings and one of the famous "Purple People Eaters." Marshall also did not like to train in the offseason. His comment was, "There's only so much tread on a tire."] Yep, that was Paul Johnson."

OFFENSIVE LINEMEN/GUARDS:

Conor Crimmins (1999-'02) played his freshman and sophomore seasons for Sully and became one of Carleton's most highly decorated talents at guard. Conor received all three of the football trophies. He won the Zell in 2000, and C.J. Hunt in 2001. In his final year, he was All-MIAC, took home the Lippert, and was a team captain.

"Conor was all-everything in high school. He was always a leader, captain of everything in high school, and played in a high school all-star game. I started him out at tackle, but he was a natural guard, and we moved him to guard eventually, where he succeeded and excelled much better than he did at tackle. He played for me two seasons, with his sophomore season in 2000 being my last at Carleton."

Paul Kane (1996-'99) played only one season with Conor Crimmins, but they had similar career trajectories. Both were immediate contributors and demonstrated toughness and leadership throughout. Paul made the All-MIAC second team in 1998 and '99. In his senior season, he won the Lippert and served as a team captain.

"Paul had a similar story as Crimmins. Captain of his high school team in Bloomington, Minnesota, played in the year-end all-star game. Both great players who started immediately as freshman; both played all four years. Paul was a great leader. Very emotional kid, he wanted to win, he wanted to win very badly. He's one of those guys that after game, he cried, more than once. And I think he expected more out of himself. He was always giving 100% and was clearly one of the best guards that we ever had."

Tommy Olsen (1984-'88) was an incredibly stalwart and consistent player who rarely made a mistake on the offensive line. He was somewhat undersized but extremely strong. Tommy won the Lippert Award in 1988 and was a team captain in both 1987 and '88.

"Tommy was one of my three best at guard. He was actually smaller and more slender than a typical offensive guard but he was incredibly strong and tough. He held his own just fine. He was smart as hell and a great leader, team captain and all that good stuff."

OFFENSIVE LINEMEN/CENTERS:

Geoff Morse (1989-'92) was the best center who ever played for Sully. He was intelligent but also football smart. He was versatile and rarely made mistakes. Geoff was named All-America and All-MIAC as a key cog in the 1992 championship team.

"Geoff was out of Utah. He was an All-American for us. Missed his freshman year with injury, didn't play that year. But started from there on out. He was just outstanding as a center, and he called the defenses. Blocked everything in front of him and could move well because of his good feet. Highly, highly intelligent football player and leader. Never had to coach him. Just had to tell him once and then he had it down pat. I remember he was very impressed with Carleton when he first got here as a freshman. He was amazed at how quickly our kids adapted to everything. He was very surprised, apparently from his high school experience, at the level of football IQ of our players.

And he fit right into that, of course. As a center you have to do a lot of different things besides snap the football and he could do everything you wanted him to do."

Tim Kruse (1979-'80) was a two-year wonder, whose promising career was cut short by injury. But he made a huge impression while he played, being named All-MIAC as a freshman in 1979, and winning the Zell in 1980.

"Tim was only with us two years. He had a concussion, had to give up the game. He was one of the first recruits I had. He was out of Colorado. He was really good. He was an immediate starter and a dominant center for those two years he played. He was All-Conference as a freshman and just really talented from the get-go. Great attitude, great leader, very vocal leader. He had phrases which I'm forgetting, which I should remember. They were pretty good, and he would relay those on to the offensive lineman and they would respond in kind. Just a rock-solid player."

Steve Ford (1980-'83) was known for his quiet consistency, winning attitude, and team leadership. He received the Zell in 1981 and was named All-MIAC in 1982.

"Steve was Billy Ford's younger brother [Bill Ford, 1978-'81, starred at quarterback and is a C-Club Hall of Famer] and a solid performer. He was a smart football player, very coachable and a leader, both on and off the field. He was a multi-year starter at center. He never made any mistakes, just did his job, every down. He had a great, optimistic kind of attitude."

RUNNING BACKS

Adam Henry (1990-'93) was Sully's all-time ball carrier. He was All-MIAC for three straight years starting in 1991. He was an All-America Honorable Mention and won the C.J. Hunt in 1992. He was team MVP in 1992 and '93 and won the Lippert in 1993. Adam was third all-time in scoring upon graduation, with 168 career points. He was first in season all-purpose offense (rushing, receiving and kick/punt return yards) with 2,035 yards in 1992, as well as first in career all-purpose offense with 6,151 yards. Adam is Carleton's leader in career rushing yards with 3,482, and in career rushing TDs with 26. Adam is a member of the C-Club Hall of Fame.

"Adam was the best ever. Of course, his numbers are amazing. Almost every game he played was a 100-yard rushing game. He was a great punt and kick returner. Very fast, in fact, extremely fast. He was on a relay team that won a MIAC championship. He just was so damn good. It's hard to explain. He was solid. He was the best back in the MIAC his last two years, for sure. He was hurt during his freshman year and missed a couple of games. He was a teammate of Ted Kluender in high school at South Saint Paul, and the two of them were their best players at South Saint Paul, and they were here too. Adam could catch the football coming out of the backfield, as a receiver. His speed was his forte. He also had great vision, and his numbers speak for themselves, they are off the charts."

Dan Neinhuis (1983-'86) became the first player in Carleton football history to eclipse the 1,000-yard rushing mark and Carleton's first recipient of the MIAC MVP award in 1986. He was the 1984 Zell winner and received All-MIAC honors in 1985 and 1986. In '86, he led the conference in scoring, rushing yards, punt return yards, and all-purpose yards. When he graduated, Dan owned the top figures in recorded team history for single-season rushing yards (1,044), single-season all-purpose yards (1,786), career all-purpose yards (4,552), and season and career punt and kickoff return average and total return yards. Dan was inducted into the C-Club Hall of Fame in 1997.

"Dan was a character. He loved the game, he was very vocal, and a fun-loving guy. Football for him was a joy. He just had fun playing, laughing all the time. There was nothing he didn't think he could do. He was supremely confident, and his numbers were outstanding. He was MVP of the conference. He was the best back in the league for two years at least. Very fast, he was a high stepper. He was a great receiver coming out of the backfield. As with Adam Henry, Dan's career numbers were just outstanding."

Skye Flanagan (1994-'97) was a superb running back, and a workhorse who set the Carleton record by carrying the football an astounding 49 times in a game against St Olaf in 1997. Skye was All-MIAC and team captain in 1996 and 1997, as well as team MVP in '97. Skye holds the individual record for a single game, scoring five TDs for 30 points vs. St. Thomas in 1996. He also holds the single season record, scoring 94 points in 1996. Skye finished his career with 2,271 rushing yards and 15 rushing TDs.

"Skye was another running back with great numbers. He was a Montana kid. Really enthusiastic guy. He couldn't wait to get the football. He was always 'give me the ball,' you know, and he had the record for most carries; I think in one game he carried the ball close to 50 times. He had several 100-yard games. Fast, aggressive. But his attitude made him good. I mean, he was good anyway, but his attitude made him good. He wanted the football and once he got it, he was going somewhere with it. People in the league respected him too. A lot. He got a lot of compliments from opposing coaches for his desire and his hard running."

WIDE RECEIVERS

Jim Bradford (1988-'91) was a three-time All-American. When he graduated, his 3,719 receiving yards ranked third all-time in Division III history. At the completion of his career, Bradford held MIAC records for receiving yards in a game (285), receiving yards in a season (1,238), yards in a career (3,719), catches in a game (13), catches in a career (214) and touchdown receptions in a season (13). His 32 career touchdown catches still stand as Carleton's all-time record. His 196 career points scored is also a school record. Jim is in the C-Club Hall of Fame.

"Three-time All-American. I don't know what else you could say about him. Led the league in pass receiving for all those years. He was out of Idaho. A kid who was all everything in Idaho, but too small, too slow, they said for Division I, whatever. And we got him. He wasn't 6 feet, he was 5-10 maybe. He had what I considered good speed. But great hands and great at running routes. He played the game with tremendous enthusiasm and confidence and just had a natural knack for catching the ball and running with it. For him to catch the football was one thing, but after that you couldn't get him. He was a great kickoff return specialist. He was a good blocker too. His numbers speak for themselves. His abilities helped us win a lot of football games. He even came and coached with us a year after he left also."

John Winter (1981-'84) finished his career with 99 receptions for 1,702 yards and 16 touchdowns. When he graduated, he held school records for most catches in a game (11), reception yardage in a game (190) and for most catches, reception yardage and touchdown receptions in a single season. He was named the team's MVP in 1984. He still holds the school record for longest reception, 99 yards, in a 1983 game against Trinity, Texas (a record which will, of course, never be broken). John was also an outstanding All-America sprinter in track and field and was voted into the C-Club Hall of Fame in 2005.

"John was a great recruit for us out of Indiana. His recruiting process was interesting for me because I hadn't known about him initially, and Hank Whitman, who was in the admissions office at the time said, 'By the way, I've run across an application from this kid from Indiana. Looks like he might be a player,' and he said his name is John Winter, so I went in and got the file. Oh, yeah, no kidding. He's All-State. And I'm thinking, 'Why is he applying to Carleton in the first place?' Well, part of the reason was he was an A student, and he wasn't very big. He was like 5-10 or 11. Very fast, ran on the track team. Set several kinds of records in track. He was small, but fast, great hands, ran extremely well, was not known as a great blocker. We put him in motion all the time for two reasons, first, to isolate him one-on-one with the D-backs and second, he wasn't going to block anybody, so by putting him in motion, he didn't have to. Two guys had to cover him, so that's better than a block. And he had great numbers. He made the winning catch in the Miracle at Ripon game [in 1981 Carleton came back from a 21-3 fourth quarter deficit to defeat Ripon; the Knights' final drive went 97 yards and ended with a leaping TD catch by freshman John Winter.] Caught it up between two guys, jumped up. He could really jump, too. Even though he wasn't tall, I can't tell you how many touchdowns he scored that way, but it was plenty."

Jeff Scherer (1988-'91) possessed blazing speed and may well have been the fastest athlete in Carleton history. He was a four-time All-American sprinter in track and field. He earned the MIAC's most valuable athlete award in 1992. As a football receiver, he made 119 career catches. He totaled 2,153 career receiving yards with 26 touchdowns. He earned All-America honorable mention honors in 1991 with 29 catches for 704 yards and six touchdowns, including a 98-yard touchdown. Jeff is a C-Club Hall of Famer.

"Those guys [Scherer and Bradford] were the two best receivers in the league. Jeff was from Nebraska. The key word with him is fast. He was tall and lanky. Sprinter. Won the MIAC in the 100 and 200 meters, two years in a row. He and Bradford

together were an awesome pair. Not only was Jeff a good receiver but he was a good blocker too. He was a true split end. We didn't put him in motion like we did John Winter, and Bradford occasionally. But Jeff could catch the football and obviously run with it. He could do it all and as I say, speed was the name of his game."

TIGHT ENDS

Scott Hanks (1989-'92) was a captain of the 1992 championship team. He began his football career at running back, then transitioned to tight end for his senior season. Scott became an All-MIAC performer at his new position and led the nation in receptions by a tight end with 63, earning All-America Honorable Mention. Scott made the C-Club Hall of Fame in 2008.

"Scott was out of Hopkins High School; his dad was a coach there. He was a running back for us for three years. And a good running back. But in '92 we had other good running backs. We thought when we were looking for a tight end that Scott would be a natural. As a running back he also was a very good receiver coming out of the backfield, so we moved him to tight end, and he became an All-American. He could run that wheel route. He could run crossing routes; he could block a little bit also. And he was just an absolute natural and obviously the best tight end we ever had for sure. But that running back background helped him as a tight end. He made several big catches that helped us win football games and for the championship team in 1992, he led the nation in number of catches for a tight end."

Brian Davies (1976-'79) was a local kid who grew up in Faribault, Minnesota. He had a quiet toughness and was highly respected as a team leader. He was a big, incredibly versatile player who starred on offense, defense, and special teams as a punter. Brian won the Lippert, was All-Midwest Conference, and was a team captain for Sulley's inaugural 1979 championship squad.

"Brian was there when I got there. I think he went to Bethlehem Academy High School there in Faribault. He was a senior in '79. He was one of the best players that I inherited when I got there, if not the best player. He was a captain, and he played both ways, offensively at tight end and defensively as an end. He also had a great leg as a punter. Big tough kid, aggressive, and had a little bit of a mean streak. He could do everything I wanted from the tight end in terms of catching the ball. His leadership

was obvious. He was kind of a clutch player. If you needed something in the clutch offensively, you could count on him to get free and catch the football. He's another one of those guys that had a sort of quiet off the field demeanor, but he was mean in football pads."

Brad McDowell (1991-'94) had all the attributes to become one of Sully's best tight ends. He was a fine all-around athlete who excelled as a kicker, punter and long snapper too. He won the C.J. Hunt Trophy and was All-MI-AC as the top tight end in the conference in 1993. Brad caught 55 balls for 814 yards in his career.

"Brad was out of Wayzata, Minnesota. He was a natural with all the things you would possibly look for in a tight end. Size, speed, hands, great hands. He was an absolute natural and he was a heck of a punter too. He started all three years, maybe four. All-Conference. Top tight end of the league junior year. He was enthusiastic, with a very positive attitude. He did exceptionally well in that area of positive reinforcement."

QUARTERBACKS

Tim Nielson (1985-'88) was a three-time All-MIAC quarterback in football and a three-time All-MIAC baseball catcher and infielder. He was a 1988 All-American and MIAC MVP on the gridiron. He compiled 5,606 yards of total offense for his career, including the MIAC single-game record of 508 yards against Gustavus Adolphus. He also led Carleton to four successive victories against St. Olaf in Goat Trophy games. Tim entered the C-Club Hall of Fame in 1999. His jersey number, lucky 13, is the only Carleton football jersey ever to be retired.

"Tim was the best player of all time in my career. He was the player of the year in the state of Montana. He was in Sports Illustrated as a high school player. Came to Carleton in large part because he was 5 foot 8. He wasn't even 5 foot 10. But strong as heck. Very strong physically. Fast, extreme quickness, high in football IQ. That was off the charts. We were an option team at the time. He could run the option better than anybody in Division I as far as I'm concerned. Good passer, great baseball player. Also, his sister had been at Carleton, and she influenced his coming. Tim was an art major.

He was a little bit different personality-wise. One of the reasons he said he came to Carleton was he liked our helmets. And so anyway, one way or another, we got him, and we started him at running back at first because we had a senior quarterback. We finally moved him to QB later, which I should have done right away, but he did a great job as a running back too. Great leader, smart as hell, football-wise. And off the field, of course, as well. He was like some of those other guys too. He's quiet, but once he played football, he had a mean streak. He was aggressive and very tough. He didn't shirk from any contact, I'll tell you that."

John Nielson (1987-'90) also excelled in both football and baseball. He was a two-time All-America in baseball. In football, he achieved career totals of 4,611 yards passing and 5,343 yards of total offense. He threw 44 touchdowns in only two years as a starting quarterback. He was a two-year captain, and he was named All-MIAC first team in 1989 and 1990. He led the conference in passing and total offense in both of those seasons. John joined his brother in the C-Club Hall of Fame in 2001.

"His brother John was the exact opposite of Tim, personality-wise. John was the better passer of the two, but also a good runner and John was a great baseball player. He was an All-American in baseball. There was nothing that he didn't think he could do. He wasn't afraid of anything, just like his brother wasn't either. John played defense. In fact, in his first two years when Tim was the quarterback, John was one of the safeties. He did a heck of a job as a defensive back. He set all kinds of records as a quarterback, his junior and senior years, and was a captain. John also came back after graduation and played baseball, as did Tim, in the summer amateur baseball leagues here in Minnesota."

Ted Kluender (1989, '91-'93) was a stellar, strong-armed passer and one of the key leaders on the '92 championship team. Ted won the Zell in 1991 and was co-recipient of the Lippert (with his buddy Adam Henry) and a team captain in 1993. Ted threw for 486 yards and five touchdowns in a game against Bethel in 1991. He had 1,938 passing yards in 1992. Ted threw for 5,058 career yards and 50 TDs, which when he graduated put him first all-time in those categories.

"Teddy was out at South Saint Paul with Adam Henry. They came together. A

blessing for me and for Carleton football. Teddy had a great arm. Threw the ball really well. Not much of a runner. But a good passer and a good play caller. Very self-confident. A good leader, team captain. He took a year off to go to junior college but then came back. Thankfully so. He led the championship team in '92. Led the league in everything in his junior year but got hurt in his senior year and missed several games. Great player. Teddy was the leader of that bunch then, and he still is. Ever since he graduated, he's been very much a supporter of Carleton football and involved in everything as an alum. He's been a real leader off the field, particularly socially of all things; in terms of weddings and parties and fishing trips and things like that, Teddy was always there, leading the way."

KICKERS

Pat Bell (1989-'90, '92) was a fine, consistent kicker who scored 123 career points. He was third on the career list with 15 field goals (15-28). He was number one all-time in career extra points, and was literally automatic, making all 76 of his attempts.

"Pat was just a kicker for us. He didn't play anything else, and he was an automatic kicker. Solid. Never had to worry about him. Should we kick a field goal? Yeah, wherever we were inside the 40 for sure. And the PATs were automatic. Pretty much all the time."

Dan Hedlund (1985-'88) was second all-time with 17 field goals (he went 17 for 25) and sixth all-time in extra points with 69 (69-73). Dan made four career kicks of more than 40 yards.

"Same as Pat Bell, Dan was strictly a kicker. Both of them were pure kickers Dan was incredibly reliable on kickoffs, field goals and PATs. Just a solid, dependable guy. Practiced his art. It's an art, and all three of those guys, Dave Grein, Pat Bell and Dan did not shirk practice duties. They worked on it all the time, not just Fridays."

Dave Grein (1981-'84) was an excellent defensive back but also extremely reliable as a kicker. He was sixth all time in field goals, going 13 for 20. He made 50 out of 56 career extra points for eighth all-time. Dave made a 46-yard field goal against Macalester in 1984 and won All-MIAC honors as a kicker in 1982.

"Dave was the son of a former Carleton player. Dave was a starter at defensive back, but he was also a kicker, and his numbers were very good. He was very consistent. He was just a great kicker for us. No problems. He could kick it off, hit field goals, PATs, the whole nine yards."

PUNTERS

Rusty Scott (1981-'84) was a good defensive back who also had a powerful kicking leg and was Sully's best ever as a punter. He was fifth all-time with 3,984 career punting yards. He was fifth in career attempts at 107, and his 37.23 yards per kick average was good for fourth on the career list. Rusty launched a punt 70 yards against Concordia in 1984, and another one 68 yards vs. Bethel in 1983.

"Rusty was the best punter that we ever had in my time as coach. He was from Saint Paul. His dad, Bobby Scott, played at Carleton on the undefeated 1954 team. And so did his uncle. A lot of Carleton alumni were from the Scott family. Rusty was a great punter. He had perfect form. He could hit the spiral, and he could pump it to 40 yards, 50 yards if he wanted. He could put the ball where you needed it to be. He was good. Played safety too, by the way."

Andy Quist (1995-'99) was one of the most versatile players in Carleton football history. He played quarterback on offense, was a defensive back, and an excellent punter. He won the Zell trophy in 1996, was a team captain in 1998 and 1999, and won the Lippert Award in 1999. In his career, Andy hit 107 punts for 3,481 total yards and 32.53 average yards per kick. Andy holds the record for the longest punt, booming a ball 82 yards vs. St Thomas in 1999.

"Andy was a two-way player, in fact a three-way player at that. He was out of Alexandria, Minnesota, the son of a football coach from up there. I had to recruit him hard to get him. He was a quarterback. He played defensive back. And he was a punter. He did it all. He hit a punt once, wind aided, that went over 80 yards. He was hurt one year and missed the season. One year he started in the secondary; he played all season at D-back. Another year he was my quarterback. Versatile. Talented. Could do more than one thing; he could run and pass as the quarterback. Very team-oriented leader,

captain. The kids looked to him for leadership, and he gave it to them."

Chris French (1992-'96) was the lone freshman regular on the Knights' 1992 MIAC championship squad. By the time he graduated, he ranked second in team history with 603 career rush attempts and 2,574 career rushing yards. He totaled 20 career rushing touchdowns, spanning parts of five seasons as he missed most of 1995 due to injury. A preseason All-American at fullback in 1994, Chris went on to post his best season statistically, with 939 rushing yards on 217 carries and nine rushing touchdowns. He was also named the punter on the All-MIAC squad after posting a conference-best 37.61 yards per punt. He is third all-time with 155 career punts totaling 5,468 yards. Chris is in the C-Club Hall of Fame.

"Chris was a big-time player. He could have gone D-II easily and he was recruited by a lot of Ivy League schools. He was from Brainerd, Minnesota, and was a 4.0 student. I think Cornell flew him out there and they didn't show any cordiality to him at all, so he wasn't going to Cornell even though he could have gone Ivy League. And so anyway, we got the guy, I think he chose us for academics, and he knew he could play right away, which he did. On that '92 championship team Chris started right away at running back and as a punter. But he was a great running back. A very good punter, obviously. We had some fake punts with him, of course, because he could throw it too."

KICK/PUNT RETURNERS

Adam Henry is second all-time with 1,743 yards on 88 career kick returns. He averaged 19.81 yards per kick return, for thirteenth place all-time.

Dan Neinhuis is sixth on the all-time kick-return list with 1,171 career yards on 56 returns. He is sixth on the career list with 20.91 yards per kick return. Dan is first in career punt return yards with 532 yards on 48 returns, and he ripped off a 77-yard punt return vs. Augsburg in 1986.

Dan Reider (1997-'00) was a versatile player who could both catch and run with the football. He was All-MIAC in his senior season. He is third on the all-time kick return list with 1,448 total yards on 79 career returns. He averaged 18.33 yards per kick return in his career and scored a kick return touchdown of 87 yards against Concordia in 1997. Dan also returned a record 68 punts for 381 yards (third all-time) in his career.

"Dan was a compact guy out of Blaine, Minnesota. He was a wide receiver and running back. Good football player. We went to Germany when he was here and he was the star of the German trip, but as a kick returner. He just had that vision, and he broke a couple of long runs and touchdowns and all that sort of thing, one of which is in our record book."

ATHLETE

Scott Klein (1993-'96) was a four-year starter and a three-time All-MIAC linebacker. He registered 359 career tackles, a school record. He graduated with the record for most tackles for losses (37) and ranked third when he left Carleton with 17 career sacks. Scott shared the program's Zell Award his sophomore season and the Hunt Trophy his junior year. He earned the Lippert Award his senior year and team MVP his junior and senior seasons. Scott is a C-Club Hall of Famer who was inducted in 2007.

"Scott was what I call a hybrid. He was All-Conference for three years in a row in the MIAC, and he was our leading tackler for three years in a row. He would never get on a scale for me. He didn't want me to know how small he really was. He was listed at 6 feet and 190. Apparently, he never was that big, but he was very, very fast, quick and hungry, and he was a hitter. He was a stalker. I mean, he could elude any block anybody tried to put on him. Forget it. He was the best blitzer we've ever had from outside. Against St. John's, one time, I think he made 22 tackles in the game. Lots of tackles for losses. He came out of Apple Valley with his brother Eric, who was a great offensive tackle for us, and I don't know how much more I can say about him, except he was phenomenal at what he did, which I considered to be a different kind of linebacker, strong safety, whatever you want to call him. He had a talent that nobody else had, and he was probably 5-10, maybe 180 I suppose, but very fast with hunger and tenacity. He had a mean streak, loved to hit people."

Legacy*

"Through our great good fortune, in our youth, our hearts were touched with fire. It was given to us to learn at the outset that life is a profound and passionate thing."

OLIVER WENDELL HOLMES, JR.

"As for my legacy, one important thing is that I hope they would say they had fun playing football, that they enjoyed playing for me. I hope they realize what a once-in-a-lifetime opportunity it was to play this beautiful game. Football is simply the greatest game there is."

BOB SULLIVAN

John Nielson, '91: "I have had so many interactions with college football players from other schools since my time at Carleton. None, not one, has ever spoken of an experience like we had. Somehow, we became a family. We knew all our teammates and many who came before or after us. There was no hazing. There was lots of time spent together (eating, watching film or movies, lifting, practicing). The bonds were almost instant. These are guys

---

* *Some of this Epilogue's quotes from Sully's players were gathered in early 2025; others are from the scrapbook assembled by the 1979 team in 2008.*

that we can still pick up with in an instant after not seeing them for years and years (something my kids point out to me every time it happens - they also think that everyone from the team they meet is cool and interesting as well!)

It was never talked about like a family. The cliches of team building were limited. Could it have been partly a Carleton thing, sure. But there were years of athletes that did not experience that in football. The only thing I could consistently tie to that super rare experience was Sully. Maybe it was more that it was a whole family experience for the Sullivans. They got 20-ish new siblings and kids each year in the family. I imagined that it helped Sully do that year in and year out. Of course that was not a direct football thing, but it put into perspective what football at Carleton under Coach Sullivan was like. It was more than just football. That is so much of what made it, and him, so special. I am grateful for that so often.

I think the thing I enjoyed the most was when Sully would laugh. The laugh when he really laughed hard. He was so energetic all the time. So earnest. Such a cool way to be in the world."

Andy Martin, '96: "As for Sully stories, I recently came across a note I wrote to my second daughter when she was less than a year old (she is now 11). In the note, which is filled with life advice, I ended with a story about something I had to memorize in college - and something that had stayed with me for all my years: the poem by Heartsill Wilson, 'A New Day.' Sully didn't inventthis but his willingness to look outside for solutions and continually improve was one of his strengths.

I also loved his sense of humor. As we aged and gained progress in the program, Sully adeptly slid the partition between coach and friend. By the end of many players' tenures, he was more than just a coach. In these times he was likely to whisper something absolutely hilarious or deadly true to you that no coach would normally share. The humanity in his ability to balance the nuance of a relationship struck me at the time and is something I've tried to carry on. There are times in life to let down the cover of seniority, superiority, title, and role and just appreciate the humor that is as we overlap with others in our brief existence."

Ryan Beckers, '94: "Sully's ability to engender a family, as opposed to merely assembling a roster, was unmatched in my experience playing team sports. The people he brought in, and the atmosphere he created, let a lot of smart kids from a lot of different backgrounds be themselves and yet be all-in for a cause. It was a wonderful kind of Kool-Aid he got us to drink, and from the moment I stepped on campus I started making lifetime friends. This translated, I think, pretty directly to competitive winning teams.

Coach Bob Sullivan was not an intimidating presence. He did not abuse or abrade; rather, he welcomed and praised or poked when necessary. I'm sure that over decades of coaching, he had detractors. But overall, what he built inspired a deep kind of love and regard, the kind that allowed for communication both ways. He was as much OUR coach as we were HIS players, and the field that was eventually named in his honor was a place where we could all be in the moment, together."

Bob Sullivan: *"I tried to instill a sense of the importance of organization and discipline and setting goals for yourself. There was a reason practice started at 3:29 p.m. You need to develop a plan and then work that plan. People who do this succeed in life."*

Troy Ethen, '88: "I applied many of Coach Sullivan's philosophies and approaches to my business career. The Psychology of Winning was omnipresent in my leadership of teams though perhaps more nuanced than prescribed. I implemented goal setting for the Company [Troy is the President and CEO of Protean Construction Products, Inc.] with cascading goals for departments and weekly scorecards all based upon Coach Sullivan's Friday goal card that included Team Goals, Unit Goals (Defense), Group Goals (D-line) and Personal Goals for each game. I came across many iterations of goal setting in leadership seminars, 'how to' business books, etc. But it started with Sully's approach. Sully also taught me to let individuals flourish in their own style. As long as there was adherence to values, including teamwork, the approach taken by the individual (the how) was less important than their contribution to the team (the what)."

Todd (Elmo) Wright, '84: "I arrived at Carleton early in August of '80 to start my Carleton experience and to try and make the football team. At the end of the season, Sully told us we would all meet with him one on one to make plans for the off season and the next season. As part of that process, he asked us to make a list of the top 10 priorities in our lives and what we wanted to accomplish in the next year and the next 5 years.

I arrived at my meeting with my lists. They included the following ideas with football on both lists and somewhere in the top 5 on both lists:

-1) family, support

-2) football and prep for next season

-3) schoolwork and course planning

-4) major select by end of year Business/Econ vs Biology

-5) develop new friends and support existing friends

-6) summer job/internship plans

-7) volunteer work at hospital in hometown during winter break and summer

…. Through 10.

I proudly handed it to Sully and he quickly glanced down the list. He smiled, then laughed as he handed it back to me. He looked me square in the eye and said, 'You know you play football at DIII Carleton in the Midwest Conference, right?' I answered a simple, 'Yes'. He said, 'Then why is football in the top 5 of your 1-year plan and why is it even on your 5-year plan? Nobody has ever made it to the pro level from Carleton and I'm pretty sure you won't be the player to break that streak.' I acknowledged his logic as he continued. 'Football at Carleton is about developing team skills, camaraderie, discipline, and making us all better persons. Football at Carleton helps you to elevate and accentuate your leadership and academic skills. So please reorganize your list and let's meet again.'

I left that meeting with the sense that I had met with a father or grandfather who was counseling me how to start living a meaningful life. Since that meeting, I have made a yearly list of goals centered on 3 ideas:

-10-15-year plan (hopes and dreams, might get 10 percent accomplished if I'm lucky)

-5-7-year plan (want to accomplish at least 50 percent of these or more)

- 1-year plan (the things I need to get done – 90 percent or more success
- to support the 5 and 10 year plans). That 'football' lesson from Sully helped guide my life."

Jamie Jurkovic, '87: "Sully's influence on my life was huge. I really wanted to play college football and Carleton was a great opportunity. I was a DIII-level guy and I wanted the best possible academics. Not sure if I would have gotten in or not without Sully. He probably recommended I apply Early Decision which was a good call.

Carleton was such a transformative experience for me, especially coming from a small mining town in Northern Minnesota as a first-generation college kid. Met my wife at Carleton. My son went to Carleton. I worked in Admissions for Carleton. And I coached football for 30 years. From middle school up through the high school ranks. Served as an assistant in a few Prep Bowls. Sully was always an influence on how to be fair, competitive, and diligent in preparation and communication and organization. All sorts of Sullyisms would pop into my vocabulary coaching football. Starting practice at :29 or :59 to emphasize being on time. Little things make a difference. 'Opportunity time' - like when there was a turnover. It's not 'ah shit time!' - it's 'opportunity time!' It's time to make a big play. That was all Sully.

Bob Sullivan: *"I tried to focus on the concept of positivity, the importance of staying positive even in the face of adversity. And the importance of perseverance. Sometimes you get your butt kicked in a football game, and in life. You have to never give up, even when that happens. You keep trying, you keep moving forward, no matter what."*

Brent Siegel, '83: "Coach Sullivan's visionary leadership style showed me that as a leader it was important to look beyond narrow tactical success. In short, to create impact beyond mastering the tasks of that one position and to look for a way to provide bigger and more impactful results. Don't focus just on fixing a problem but rather create a whole new framework that addresses individual problems in the context of achieving a larger goal. This meant for me as a husband, father and leader that I should create something that impacted more people. I leveraged and repurposed concepts Sully taught us like visualization, the team prayer, and not dwelling on the past but instead looking forward, to shape how I have tried to lead and impact others in my life.

The thing that I have recently started to focus on is a line that he always used: 'It never rains on Carleton football.' He stuck to that line even if it was raining. It occurs to me now that he really wasn't talking about the weather. He was looking at a bigger picture, a bigger game. 'It never rains on Carleton football' was both a statement to the universe and higher powers that, in fact, it should stop raining now, and further that we as Carleton football players do not let anything deter us. We can and will overcome obstacles as if they are not even there."

Trae Monroe ,'96: "My favorite Sully story? It's not 'oh-shit' time! We all remember MANY Sullyisms: GOYA [Get Off Your Ass]; Act as if [Act as if you are a champion]; and so forth. But the one I heard the most in my career was, 'It's not oh-shit time!' Meaning when something bad happens, don't say 'oh shit' and panic or get down; rise to the occasion and make the most of it. Well, we had several young QBs my last two seasons of 1994-'95 who went on to have great careers, but had a lot of turnovers early on (26 interceptions my senior year). And I was a defensive back, so I got to run back onto the field a LOT of times with Sully yelling behind us, 'It's not oh-shit time! It's not oh-shit time!'

Fast forward to sometime around 2015 when I got to watch a game at Laird with Sully after he retired from Carleton (but was helping his son coach at Northfield). The game was back and forth and looked like it might come down to the wire. About midway through the second half our offense turned the ball over, and Sully said, 'Oh shit.' Instantly, the words I had heard SO many times from him were now coming out of my mouth: 'Coach it's not oh-shit time. It's not oh-shit time.' 'You're right! You're right!' he said grabbing me by both shoulders. A few plays later our defense got a turnover. And the game did come down to the wire, but I'm pretty sure Carleton came up short. I've applied Sullyisms to my life many times the last 33 years, and maybe the most memorable time was getting to return the favor to him!"

Karl Thomas, '83: "I grew up with a positive disposition, but had not yet developed the framework on which to best use this talent to the benefit of myself and those around me. Coach Sully's lessons of perseverance, consistency and self-empowerment helped me focus this talent and gave meaning to the idea that there is no such thing as 'ah shit time.' This philosophy has been a driving force in my life. Sully taught that all events are opportunities and what may seem like adversity today, may be the best thing to ever happen to you tomorrow. The thrill of taking the field after an offensive fumble and having the attitude that the defense will score before the offense next has that ball remains with me. I carry that thrill with me whenever I face new situations."

Bob Sullivan: *"We always treated each other with respect. If you are on our team, you are a part of it, whether you are the All-Conference star or the last guy on the bench. If we ever want to accomplish anything at all, we need to work together as a team. Nothing else matters."*

Bart Reed, '90: "During my time on the Carleton football team, I was an undersized center and not much of a player. I got into about 40% of our games, always late in a big victory (except for once in a big loss to the Johnnies, but that's not important). During one tight game against Hamline during my senior year, injuries pressed me into service during a key drive. I held my own on the field for a few plays before we figured out a better way to shuffle the line for the rest of the game.

It was after the game when Coach gave me a moment I'll never forget. After finishing the game with a close victory, Sully called out key contributors to the game. Some of them were obvious, like our amazing quarterback/receiver combo of Nielson and Bradford. But then Sully took the time to mention how broadly everyone on the team contributed, naming a little-used defensive back and a certain undersized center. The ovation we received from the team gave me one of the best feelings and fondest memories I hold. The fact that Coach Sullivan valued and appreciated the contributions of even the last guys on the bench was just one of the things that made him such a great coach and inspired the loyalty of his players."

Jon Darby, '83: "Sully was the first coach I had that 'coached up,' or provided a positive coaching style. He didn't berate me for a mistake, but pointed out what I could do differently next time. He also cared about all the players, not just the stars. As a guy who spent most of his playing time on the scout squad in practice rather than in games, and then on the sideline as a student coach after an injury, I felt just as important to Sully as the captains.

There are a ton of Sully stories that will make people laugh, but my favorite is a bit different. I came to Carleton from Montana, having never seen the Carleton campus or even been in Minnesota. Sully and fellow coach Nelly met me at the airport in Minneapolis and drove me to Northfield before two-a-days started. I was not a recruited football player and knew no one on campus. Sully and Nelly spent their time showing me I was important to the team, even as an undersized 17-year-old freshman, just simply by picking me up at the airport."

John Gnaedinger, '83: "Having just been accepted at Carleton 'Early Decision,' I had already begun trying to figure out what I might be taking, wondering who my roommate would be, what college life would be like, etc., when the phone at my house rang one evening. It was Coach Sullivan, who, I guess, had heard that I had played three years of high school football. He was 'recruiting' me to play for Carleton. For a guy who thought his football days were over, who didn't really possess the skills and athleticism of a collegiate athlete, the simple concept that a college coach was actually *recruiting* me had a meaningful and lasting impact on me.

My playing time was limited, my skills were nothing compared to the other guys on the field, and I knew that, but Coach Sullivan always made me feel like a contributor and a valued member of the team. I have great memories of my brief career, that first year, 1979, none of which would have been possible without that one very important phone call from my coach. I thank Coach Sullivan for everything he did for all of us. It all made a difference in my life, and in the lives of countless others who Coach no doubt impacted similarly."

Bob Sullivan: *"At the end of the day my guys, the guys who played for me, will say what my legacy was, not me."*

Your guys have spoken, Coach. Your legend and legacy will be secure long after you are gone from this Earth. Thank you for all you have done to make us better men, husbands, fathers, friends, leaders, citizens. Oh, and we also had a helluva lot of fun playing football for you. We were touched with fire in our youth and learned that life is a profound and passionate thing, because of you. We love you. Godspeed Sully!

Amen

ACKNOWLEDGMENTS

To Coach Sullivan for agreeing to allow me the honor of writing his life story, and for generously giving of his time and archival materials. The many hours we spent together were priceless, and I could not have done it without you, Sully. To the Sullivan family: Stacy, Tim, Bubba, and Molly, thanks for sharing great family stories. A special shoutout and thank you to Bubba for your editorial help (it's always good to have an English teacher review your writing.) To my brother and teammate from the long-ago football wars, Steve Huffer, for skillful editorial, proofreading and fact-checking assistance – thanks Huff. To current Carleton linebacker Jackson LeBlanc for assiduous work in putting the index together the old-fashioned way: manually. Thank you young warrior.

To the following loyal Knights who provided the generous financial support that made this project possible: Danal Abrams, Dave Adams, Kevin Collier, Jon Darby, Brian Davies, Guy Finne, Jim Haughn, Dan Hedlund, John Heyneman, Dave Hoppe, Steve Huffer, Bob Jacobson, Andy Martin, Paul Moore, Tommy Olsen, Scott O'Reilly, Pete Ross, Brent Siegel, Scott Wilhelmy, John Winter, Curt Wyffels, and John Youngblood. Thank you, gentlemen, for stepping up when we needed you. To all the guys who sat for interviews or answered written questions, your stories and recollections of Coach were fantastic. Thank you.

To Amy Quale and the excellent team at Wise Ink Creative Publishing, thanks for helping me produce Book Number Seven (!). To Emily Rodvold, my design genius, for another stellar effort.

To my wife Faith and our daughters Anna and Lucia, for your never-ending support and encouragement. I will love you always.

PHOTOS

Front cover photo: Coach Sullivan in mid-career on the football grid-iron at Laird Stadium that would one day bear his name; Back flap photos: top: the author striking the Heisman pose on the future Bob Sullivan Field at Laird Stadium in the fall of 1979; bottom: the author finishing a 60-yard dash on the indoor track (no longer in existence) at Laird Stadium in the winter of 1977-78; Back cover photos, starting top left and moving left to right: Sully's first group of seniors, fall 1979; top row, left to right: Steve Huffer (Huff); Brian Davies (BD); Brad Schultz (Schwartz), (deceased); Phil Keithan (Monty); Zak Helmerich (Z-Dog); Tom Woodward (Woody), (deceased); front row, left to right: Tim Sommerfeld (Sommer), (deceased); Mark Timmerman (Timmer); Scott Wilhelmy (Scooter); Jeff Appelquist (App); Eric Moe (E-Moe); Mike Sullivan (Snake); Tim Franz (Franzie); Coach Sully, Zen master and football mad scientist, at work in his laboratory; Bob and Shirley Sullivan on their wedding day, December 26, 1957; Coach Bubba Sullivan, Coach Bob Sullivan, and author Jeff Appelquist in front of Sully's boyhood home, 310 First Street, Marshall, Minnesota, in December 2024 (photo taken by Kathy Flanary); Sully is triumphantly carried off the field as Carleton wins the MIAC title with a stirring victory over Gustavus on November 14, 1992; the Sullivan family upon Bob's retirement from coaching at Carleton, left to right: Molly, Stacy, Shirley, Bob, Tim, and Bubba; Bob Sullivan, basketball star at Central Catholic High School in Marshall, circa-1950s.

BIBLIOGRAPHY

American Football Coaches Association. *Defensive Football Strategies*. Illinois, Human Kinetics, 2000.

American Football Coaches Association. *The Football Coaching Bible*. Illinois, Human Kinetics, 2002.

American Football Coaches Association. *Football Coaching Strategies*. Illinois, Human Kinetics, 1995.

American Football Coaches Association. *Offensive Football Strategies*. Illinois, Human Kinetics, 2000.

Axman, Steve. *Attacking Modern Defenses with the Multiple-Formation Veer Offense*. New York, Parker Publishing Company, Inc., 1978.

Bernstein, Ross. *Pigskin Pride: Celebrating a Century of Minnesota Football*. Minnesota, Nodin Press, 2000.

Belichick, Bill. *The Art of Winning*. New York, Avid Reader Press, 2025.

Billick, Brian. *The Q Factor: The Elusive Search for Elite NFL Quarterbacks and Other Great Leaders*. New York, Hatchette Book Group, 2020.

Bissinger, H. G. *Friday Night Lights: A Town, a Team, and a Dream*. Massachusetts, De Capo Press, 1990.

Bostrom, Boz. *A Legacy Unrivaled: The Story of John Gagliardi*. Minnesota, Minnesota Historical Society Press, 2016.

Carroll, Bob, Pete Palmer and John Thorn. *The Hidden Game of Football: A Revolutionary Approach to the Game and Its Statistics*. Illinois, University of Chicago Press, 2023.

Coller, Mathew. *Football is a Numbers Game: Pro Football Focus and How a Data Driven Approach Shook Up the Sport*. Illinois, Triumph Books LLC, 2023.

Crawford, Robert. *The Bard: Robert Burns: A Biography*. New Jersey, Princeton University Press, 2009.

Goldstein, Richard. *Ivy League Autumns: An Illustrated History of College Football's Grand Old Rivalries*. New York, St. Martin's Press, 1996.

Hargitt, Rich. *The RPO Bible: Offensive Game Planning and Play Calling in the Age of the RPO*. California, Coaches Choice, 2021.

Harris, David. *The Genius: How Bill Walsh Reinvented Football and Created an NFL Dynasty*. New York, Random House Publishing, 2008.

Holtz, Lou. *Wins, Losses and Lessons*. New York, Harper Entertainment, 2007.

Kirwan, Pat. *Take Your Eye Off the Ball 2.0: How to Watch Football by Knowing Where to Look*. Illinois, Triumph Books LLC, 2015.

Layden, Tim. *Blood, Sweat and Chalk: The Ultimate Football Playbook: How the Great Coaches Built Today's Game*. New York, Sports Illustrated Books, 2010.

Murphy, Austin. *The Sweet Season: A Sportswriter Rediscovers Football, Family, and a Bit of Faith at Minnesota's St. John's University*. New York, HarperCollins Publishers, 2001.

Silver, Michael. *The Why is Everything: A Story of Football, Rivalry, and Revolution*. New York, W.W. Norton & Company, Inc., 2024.

Sullivan, Bob. *Knights of the Gridiron: A History of Carleton College Football, 1883-2005*. Self-published, 2006.

Tamte, Roger R. *Walter Camp and the Creation of American Football*. Illinois, University of Illinois Press, 2018.

Thole, George and Jerry Foley. *Coaching the Veer Offense*. California, Coaches Choice, 2009.

Wacker, Jim and Don Morton. *The Explosive Veer Offense for Winning Football*. New York, Parker Publishing Company, Inc., 1980.

Waitley, Denis. *The Psychology of Winning*. New York, Berkley Books, 1979.

NAME INDEX

A

Abbott, Bud   3
Abrams, Danal   206
Adams, Dave   100, 101, 103, 182, 206
Alworth, Lance   67
Appelquist, Anna   164, 206
Appelquist, Faith   164, 206
Appelquist, Jeff   85, 89, 207
Appelquist, Lucia   164, 206
Appleyard, David   83, 96, 97
Axman, Steve   73

B

Beckers, Ryan   114, 118, 129, 199
Belichick, Bill   128,170
Bell, Pat   112, 193
Bell, Bobby   32
Beller, Randy   124
Bergquist, Jeff   59
Bernstein, Steve   65
Bertelli, Angelo   4
Beson, Warren   59, 138
Billick, Brian   68, 73
Blaik, Earl   76
Blake, William   39
Bogart, Humphrey   3
Bostrom, Boz   22, 23
Bradford, Jim   109, 112, 115, 188, 203
Bradovich, Bob   121, 126, 127
Brann, Chris   133, 137
Bronzan, Bill   66
Brown, Paul   67, 68
Brown, Myra   56

Bryant, Bear   22
Bunnell, Scott   100, 103, 109, 110, 174
Burns, Robert   38, 39, 40
Butkus, Dick   144
Byron, Lord   39

C

Cagney, Jimmy   3
Camp, Walter   54, 55, 209
Canakes, Stavros   34,162
Carey, Michael   109
Carleton, William   56
Carlson, Greg   37
Carnegie, Andrew   92
Cash, Roseann   43
Cash, Johnny   43, 158
Chaney, Newcomb   57
Christiansen, Jim   97
Churchill, Winston 49
Clark, William   165
Coleman, Aston   117
Coleridge, Samual Taylor   39
Collier, Kevin   206
Confucius   161
Cooper, Edwin   33
Cooperider, Ben   148
Costello, Lou   3
Cover, Rick   32
Cox, Aaron   118
Crawford, Robert   40
Crimmins, Conor   184
Curtis, Jack   152

D

Dandurand, Ted   14
Darby, Jon   51, 121, 122, 124, 204, 206
Davies, Brian   85, 88, 90, 190, 183, 206

Davis, Al   67, 68
DeBartolo, Eddie   68
Dean, Dizzy   116
Dent, Richard   79
Dimond, Tyler   151
Dougherty, Peggy   23
Dow, James   56

E

Earp, Wyatt   88
Eastwood, Clint   44
Edwards, Robert   58, 59, 84, 163
Edwards, Ben   104, 107
Emtman, Steve   78
Engel, Andy   88, 176, 177
Ethen, Troy   94, 99, 103, 106, 107, 175, 199
Exner, Max   56

F

Falk, Peter   25
Ferry, Steve   34
Ferry, Tom   101
Flanagan, Skye   130, 132, 187
Flanary, Kathy   160, 207
Foley, Jerry   71
Ford, Steve   186
Ford, Billy   87, 88, 89, 96, 186
Franz, J.J.   133, 175, 176, 181
Franz, Tim   85, 88, 89, 175, 207
French, Chris   116, 130, 132, 195

G

Gagliardi, John   17, 18, 19, 20, 22, 23, 24, 26, 29, 61, 66, 74, 98, 117, 135
Gagliardi, Johnny   24
Gillette, Mike   136
Gilliland, Art   112, 114, 118, 181
Gilman, Sid   67, 68

Gnaedinger, John   204

Goebel, John   32

Grant, Mike   176

Grant, Bud   176

Graupman, Tom   142

Grein, Dave   96, 193

Grench, Bruce   124

Groza, Lou   88

Gruman, Pete   93

Gunnarson, Dave   177

Guthrie, Arlo   43

H

Haberman, John   99, 101, 103, 107, 110, 178, 179

Hadl, John   67

Hampton, Dan   79

Hanks, Greg   85

Hanks, Scott   112, 116, 117, 190

Harmon, Bruce   35

Harris, Emmylou   43

Harris, David   66

Hart, Leon   4

Haughn, Jim   206

Hayes, Woody   22, 139

Heath, Jake   148

Heckroth, Jeff   143

Hedlund, Dan   193, 206

Helmerich, Zak   85, 88, 207

Henry, Adam   113, 114, 116, 118, 129, 186, 187, 192, 195

Heyneman, John   100, 103, 107, 179, 206

Hilleman, Eric   148

Hoffman, Matt   129, 131, 180

Holtz, Lou   61, 62, 63, 64, 65, 70, 75, 77

Holtz, Beth   63, 64

Hope, Bob   3

Hoppe, Dave   100, 103, 105, 107, 206

Hornung, Paul   145

Horton, Johnny   158

Hoyt, Bill   88

Huffer, Steve   87, 168, 183, 206, 207

Hunt, C.J.   56, 117, 172, 176, 178, 179, 180, 184, 186, 191

J

Jackson, Alan   43

Jacobs, Tom   109

Jacobson, Bob   206

James, Jesse   1

James, Don   78

Jennings, Waylon   43, 158

John, Pope   5

Johnson, Dan   35

Johnson, Paul   184

Jones, Ernest   56, 57

Jordan, Michael   112

Journell, Tom   138, 150, 151, 168

Journell, Mack   138

Jurkovich, Jamie   107, 157, 158, 201

K

Kalland, Guy   99, 107

Kane, Paul   131, 184

Kant, Emmanuel   3

Keats, John   39

Keith, Toby   43, 44

Keithan, Phil   85, 207

Keller, Earl   57

Kelly, Chip   83

Kemppainen, Elmer   37

Kent, Maurice   57

Kinsella, Tom   32

Kirwan, Pat   151, 169

Klein, Scott   129, 131, 196

Kluender, Ted   112, 114, 115, 117, 129, 130, 157, 187, 192

Knight, Jim   35

Knox, Chuck   144

Kohlan, Rick   96

Kowalewski, Mike   148

Krause, Paul   182

Kristofferson, Kris   43

Kruse, Tim   85, 186

Kuss, Todd   95, 177, 178

L

Lambert, Arthur   12

La-Salle, Jean-Baptiste de   29

Layden, Tim   68, 79

Leahy, Frank   4, 62

LeBlanc, Jackson   206

Lewis, Meriwether   165

Lindenkugel, Dick   58

Lombardi, Vince   170

Lorentzen, Bob   35

Lorentzen, Jim   35, 36

Ludwig, Roger   32

Lujack, Johnny   4

Lund, David   104, 107

Lunder, Leon   97

M

Mackin, Bob   51, 93

Madden, John   145

Marino, Dan   35

Marshall, Jim   184

Martin, Andy   198, 206

McAuliffe, Dick   58

McDowell, Brad   114, 191

McMichael, Steve   79

McNally, John   20

McNamara, Jack   141

Merkle, Kevin   141

Moe, Erik   85, 88, 89, 207
Moe, Tom   162
Mohrig, Jerry   58
Monroe, Trae   202
Montana, Joe   69
Moore, Paul   179, 206
Morse, Geoff   109, 185
Morton, Don   73
Moven, Eric   53
Musgraves, Kacey   1

N

Neinhuis, Dan   98, 100, 187, 195
Nelson, Jim   85, 97
Nelson, Willie   43
Nelson, Dave   177
Nicholson, Jon   95
Nickodym, Todd   101
Nielson, John   103, 112, 113, 114, 157,192
Nielson, Tom   109, 121, 133
Nielson, Tim   101, 102, 103, 104, 107, 110, 114, 157, 191
Nikolai, Julie   148
Noyes, Joanne   160

O

O'Reilly, Scott   134, 178
Olsen, Tommy   100, 185, 206
Ostrum, Mike   96
Osborne, Tom   22

P

Pagel, Bob   138
Parcels, Bill   128
Parseghian, Ara   172
Peterson, Billy Ray   101, 177
Plank, Doug   79
Plato   83

Porter, David   124
Powell, Peter   29

Q

Quale, Amy   206
Quist, Andy   131, 133, 194
Quist, Dale   59, 60

R

Rainey, William   2
Ramler, Kurt   137, 138
Reed, Bart   203
Reider, Dan   133, 195
Reif, Jack   32
Reppmann, Yogi   133, 134
Reusse, Patrick   162
Rizik, Pete   122
Rodvold, Emily   206
Roosevelt, Theodore   54
Ross, Pete   206
Rowan, Pat   131, 174
Royal, Darrell   139
Ryan, Buddy   79

S

Sallstrom, Steve   88
Schembechler, Bo   139
Scherer, Jeff   109, 115, 189
Schlifske, John   87, 90
Schoonmaker, Tim   88
Schroeder, Josh   133, 180
Schultz, Brad   85, 207
Scoggins, Chip   75
Scott, Bob   58, 194
Scott, Rusty   194
Sebastiani, Father   19
Shanley, Tom   99

Shelley, Percy   39
Sickle, Pete   107
Sieben, John   85, 88, 96, 181
Siegel, Brent   50, 121, 125, 201, 206
Siger, Eric   148
Singletary, Mike   79
Smebakken, Ted   58
Smith, Bubba   140, 144
Solzhenitsyn, Aleksandr 104
Sommerfeld, Tim   85, 207
Stagg, Amos Alonzo   26, 55, 57, 89, 101
Stam, Mike   100, 103, 104, 105, 106, 107, 108, 109, 110, 173, 174
Stengel, Casey   120
Stevens, Nick   17
Stevenson, Robert Louis   17
Stevenson, Todd   107
Stier, Al   131, 182
Stolski, Ron   148
Stolz, Bob   32
Strong, James   56
Sullivan, Anna   6, 7, 8, 9
Sullivan, Arthur   11
Sullivan, Bubba   33, 109, 123, 136, 137, 139, 140, 141, 142, 144, 145,146, 207
Sullivan, Emmet   12
Sullivan, Linda   13
Sullivan, Lizzie   5, 10, 12
Sullivan, Lorraine   12
Sullivan, Martin   8, 10, 12
Sullivan, Mike   85, 87, 123, 207
Sullivan, Molly   5, 33, 123, 156, 158, 160, 206, 207
Sullivan, Nancy   12
Sullivan, Peter   6, 7, 8, 9, 10
Sullivan, Rosemary   12
Sullivan, Sharon   12
Sullivan, Shirley   14, 15, 23, 29, 33, 84, 93, 98, 123, 126, 127, 140, 142, 148, 154, 156, 157, 158, 159, 160, 167, 207

Sullivan, Stacy   33, 84, 155, 158, 160, 206, 207

Sullivan, Tim   33, 36, 98, 144, 155

Suprenant, Eva   12

Switzer, Barry   76

T

Tabor, Jim   36

Taube, Mel   57, 59

Taylor, Bob   85

Thelin, John   53

Thiel, Al   59

Thole, George   71

Thomas, Karl   85, 88, 96, 181, 203

Thornton, Billy Bob   28

Thull, Tim   103, 180

Thurk, Jeff   133, 175, 176

Thurnblad, Jack   120

Tillis, Pam   43

Timmerman, Mark   85, 87, 207

Tritt, Travis   43

Tuomi, Willard   85, 115

Twain, Mark   138

V

Vaaler, Paul   85, 96, 97, 98, 136

Van Valkenburg, Paul   96

Volker, Neil   118

W

Wacker, Jim   73

Waitley, Denis   46

Walsh, Bill   61, 62, 65, 66, 67, 68, 69, 70, 170

Ward, Megan   148

Warmath, Murray   173

Warner, Tom   16, 29, 30, 61

Watts, Wade   63

Wayne, John   3

Wendell Holmes, Oliver   197
Whitman, Hank   189
Wiese, Tierza   84
Wilhelmy, Scott   85, 88, 89, 121, 157, 166, 206, 207
Wilson, Heartsill   198
Winter, John   95, 96, 99, 188, 189, 190, 206
Wooden, John   11
Woodward, Tom   85, 207
Wyffels, Curt   84, 85, 157, 206

Y

Yeoman, Bill   75
Yim, Sung Yeon   121
Young, Gerald   79, 115, 178
Young, John   122
Young, Steve   69
Youngblood, John   206

Z

Zell, Matt   172

www.ingramcontent.com/pod-product-compliance
Lightning Source LLC
Chambersburg PA
CBHW021827090426
42811CB00032B/2053/J